TRAUMA!

An Open Door

For Satan

by
Paul Fernandez

with
Bill Wilkes

Trauma:An Open Door For Satan,
Paul Fernandez with Bill Wilkes
ISBN # 0-89228-115-4

Copyright ©, 1995
Impact Christian Books, Inc.
  332 Leffingwell, Suite 101,
  Kirkwood, Mo. 63122
  314-822-3309
  (Orders-Only line: 1-800-451-2708)

Scripture quotations are taken from the
New International Version unless otherwise indicated.

Cover Design: SPB Studios

Printed in the United States of America

TABLE OF CONTENTS

DEDICATION

What follows in these pages is totally attributable to the Holy Spirit. He commissioned the work to be done. He inspired the words expressed. He not only spoke the Scriptures used through the prophets, He led me to them for instruction and clarification. It was His direction, instruction, guidance and conviction that caused every occasion detailed to occur under His anointed power.

Our sincerest appreciation and thanks go out to Bill Wilkes for his criticism and editorial assistance. Also to Mary Thomas and her assistant Cherry, who did the typing on the original manuscript.

Finally, to my loving and faithful wife Eve, whose contribution is immeasurable. Everything I have written is just as much about her experience as it is about mine, because of her many hours of prayer, discernment, study and actual participation in every event described. We are full and equal partners in the Lord's work.

INTRODUCTION

The many problems of a 57-yr-old homosexual are supernaturally traced to trauma in his mother's womb. The torturous voices that keep a young man from church and society are shown to stem from when, as an infant, he was thrown towards a wall by his drunken father. The interpretation of a dream through the power of the Holy Ghost enables him to drop the false guilt he has carried and rightfully place it on his father.

A mother is shown how her son received a spirit of rage as he was conceived while she was being raped. A young man plagued with a life of drugs, alcohol and repeated acts of indecent exposure learns that it all began with traumatic experiences he had with his father and a baby sitter.

A young girl is set free of demonic oppression as she is born again and receives the baptism of the Holy Spirit. She is then instructed in how she can use this newly received God given power to free her brother and sister from the pains they have all suffered, from the abuse and abandonment up upon them by their parents.

All of these cases, plus many more, were helped greatly by the Holy Spirit working His miraculous powers through the uniquely anointed ministry of Paul and Eve Fernandez. *TRAUMA -- An Open Door For Satan* describes this working by dramatically using many scriptures as it ties the emotional encounters of trauma with the life-rending experiences of disabling demonic oppression.

No one is free of traumatic encounters. Everyone experiences these unavoidable mind challenging traumas. Neither is anyone free of the demonic attacks that often follow.

This factual account of actual experiences dramatically reveals how trauma played a role in the lives of people like

Moses, David, Saul, Mary and Peter, as well as many others in the Bible. It also shows how to probe for the source of problems, cope with them, and overcome them.

This book, which Paul feels God burdened his heart to write, presents solutions to a problem almost everyone has experienced.

No one has previously written as explicitly or to such depth on this subject. It can help many thousands find freedom from trauma-induced spiritual bondage. It can also help ministers who are called to work in the area of spiritual warfare.

CHAPTER 1

FIND THE TRAUMA

GAINING ENTRY

The initial goal of a demon is to gain entry. Jesus explains this as he tells of the demon wandering through dry places. He eventually approaches a person to determine that person's condition of receptiveness. If the condition is right, he makes his entry **(Matthew 12:44-45)**.

There are three major methods of entry used by demons. They enter by means of inherited right, they come through temptation, and they make entry during moments of trauma.

ENTRY BY INHERITANCE

Exodus 20:4-5 says that God punishes those who bow down to idols, even to the third and fourth generations. Most people seem to make all sorts of things their idols. Some are even guilty of including their church and religion in this category. Deuteronomy 23:2 extends the curse to the tenth generation of the descendants of those inflicted with the illegitimate- birth spirit. These spirits remain at least that long, unless the curse is broken and the spirits are cast out. This curse also gives demons the right of entry at the time of conception.

ENTRY BY TEMPTATION AND TRAUMA

Temptation is present in all lives. It is the most common and effective approach used by demons. It is also the most obvious and direct approach. Far less direct is for them to approach during times of trauma. Trauma is the most subtle method of demonic entry. It is quite often the means used by demonic strongmen, the demons who most negatively affect one's character and personality.

EARLY TRAUMA, EARLY ENTRY

My wife Eve and I have counseled with a great number of individuals with demonic problems. There is a certain question that we try to ask in each session. I am convinced that the Holy Spirit gave me this question. I'm sure He has given it to others, as well. When it is asked under the anointing of God, a response is prompted that enables us to discover the very instant when the most troubling spirits came into the person's life.

FIND THE TRAUMA
AND YOU FIND THE DEMON

We simply ask the person we are counseling to recall their earliest recollections. These recollections are almost always memories of traumatic experiences. We have also been prompted on these trips back into memory with visions and words of knowledge from the Lord.

I believe that I am accurate in saying that, in one hundred percent of the cases in which we have uncovered the presence of demonic oppression, we have found trauma to be an important means of entry for the evil spirits.

Our goal always is to find the spirits and cast them out. The more we know about them and how they have taken hold of a person's life, the more successful we can be in getting rid of them. We have no scientific, professional or academic qualifications to speak of. We simply try to rely on what we have gained through experience, the Word of God, and the working of the Holy Spirit in our lives.

The Apostle Peter says that Satan prowls about like a roaring lion, seeking those whom he may devour **(1 Peter 5:8)**. He does this through vast armies of highly regimented and skillfully specialized demon forces. These disembodied spirit personalities are extremely well qualified as thieves, murderers and destroyers of people's minds, bodies and lives.

THEY EVEN ENTER THE WOMB

To accomplish these terrifying ends, they must first gain entry to the mind or body. The majority of these particular demons seem to enter early in life, before people are able to respond to temptation and trauma in a rational and thoughtful way. In fact, we have found numerous cases in which entry was made while the person was still in the mother's womb! One such instance occurred with a man who had spent fifty of his fifty-seven years as a homosexual. The Holy Spirit showed me an even earlier trauma than the one which opened him to the terrible demon of homosexuality at age seven.

I told him that God was revealing to me a spirit of rejection, who had entered his life when he was physically injured in his mother's womb. He responded that his older sister had described to him a traumatic moment in which she saw their father hit their mother in the stomach while she was still carrying him prior to his birth. This was all it took for that demonic, rejecting spirit to gain entry, thus making it much easier, later on, for the homosexual spirit to enter.

Another man's mother described to us how her husband in a drunken stupor had thrown her baby son at a wall. A relative miraculously caught the infant in midair, or his life would have been snuffed out as he hit the wall. The man himself remembered his father doing the same thing to him again at age five. These traumas opened doors which led to the eventual entry of tormenting spirits, who traumatized him so terribly with voices in his mind that he had completed three stints in a mental hospital when he was brought to us at age twenty-five. This man was unable to remain in church because the voices disturbed him greatly, by speaking vile, blasphemous accusations against those around him in the service. They would also terribly distort the intent and meaning of the preaching.

FIND THE STRONGMAN FIRST

At our first session with him we found his spiritual strongmen and cast them out. Then he and his mother both received the baptism in the Holy Spirit, showing evidence of it by speaking in tongues.

When they returned for his second session, he told of a dream he had the night before. His dream was of his father, who at that point had been out of his life for years. I prayed for interpretation as he described it.

Although the father was unquestionably guilty of all sorts of physical, verbal and mental abuse, the boy blamed himself. He was tortured by a spirit of guilt. The dream was an instrument of the Lord.

DON'T LISTEN TO DEMONS

Guided by the Holy Spirit, we were able to show him how the father was the guilty party, not him. The dream helped him understand this, and he began gaining self esteem. The man was still hearing the voices, although he was coping with them. Then the Lord did a remarkable thing. The Holy Spirit spoke to me. He told me "tell him to listen to Me."

This was the breakthrough. I asked him to pray for interpretation of his own tongues, as Paul says we can do (1 Corinthians 14:13). He did. He only spoke two words, but that was a beginning. Two sessions later the man was like a new person, full of confidence and ready to begin a new life.

THEY STAY UNTIL CAST OUT

Satan uses trauma to establish footholds through which he builds lifelong bases of operations. From these bases his demons, with their varied means of tormenting tactics, perform their specialized methods of destruction. Scripture reveals this clearly.

We have discovered time and time again how the directions of people's lives have been terribly altered when a demonic spirit takes advantage of a traumatic experience to begin an oppressive strangle hold on their lives. Upon entering, the demon quickly establishes a root hold. He has no intention of leaving. He is there to stay, and he is there to steal, kill and destroy **(John 10:10)**. The only way to get rid of him and to begin to heal the effects of his attack is to drive him out through the God-given power of the Holy Spirit.

SATAN'S A LIAR

Satan loves half truths. He defied God's word when he told Eve she would not die. He spoke of a different death from the one of God's commandment. Satan spoke of mortal death, but God referred to spiritual death, as He ordered Adam and Eve not to eat the forbidden fruit. Mortal death separates soul from body.

Spiritual death separates soul from God. Eve, and Adam with her, died spiritually through disobedience. As a result, man is now born into spiritual death, so that, when we develop reason and begin to think for ourselves, we become children of Satan **(John 8:44)**.

THE RIPPLE EFFECT

Only by rebirth, made available through the regenerating power of the shed blood of Jesus Christ, are the "ripples" made to cease, that were created by our being born dead. When a pebble is thrown into a pond from the shore, there are three results. It strikes the water, it sinks beneath the surface, and the ripple or result proceeds from the point of contact out toward the shore.

So it is with a demonic attack. He strikes, he enters, and the ripples or effects of the strike often endure for generations into the future. This is true regardless of whether it comes from yielding to a direct temptation or from the subtle encroachment that frequently comes from trauma.

Once, during a service we were conducting in a church in a small southern town, a 10-year-old boy came forward from his pew leading his mother by the hand. Neither of them said anything, they just stood before us. I knelt down to the youngster's level and put my arms around him.

I prayed for him momentarily and then I led him in a sinner's prayer. He responded with conviction and sincerity. Then his mother said that he had pulled her from her pew, saying he wanted Eve to pray for him. So Eve knelt down, put her arms around him and prayed for him.

Days later we received a letter from the mother with pictures of the boy and his brother. Enclosed was a letter written by the boy himself. Eve wrote back to the mother and the child. A short time later, we received a phone call from the pastor of the church, who informed us that, just that morning, the young boy had flown into a rage, broken a window, destroyed some furniture and attacked his mother in their home. The pastor invited us to come and counsel with the mother.

We went that same day and met with the mother, and with *her* mother as well, in the pastor's office. As we probed for information an interesting past was revealed. The church knew the younger woman by a name we will call Emily, but she had signed the letter to us "Rachel" (not the actual names used). In asking about this, we discovered a dual identity. Through further probing it was brought out that, to this woman, Rachel represented all the good in her life and Emily represented all of the bad.

Rachel's natural father had left her mother when Rachel was very young. The next husband raped his stepdaughter time and time again, while her mother was at work. To keep Rachel from telling her mother, the man would lock her in a dark closet in the basement for hours at a time. Eventually he left her mother, but got Rachel to go with him by threatening to kill her and her mother if she refused. He took her to a city in a northern state, where Rachel soon met a Christian woman who brought her into her home and encouraged her to go to church. In time Rachel married.

Here we see the ripple effect in action. The trauma Rachel had experienced with her stepfather had opened the door for many spirits. Rejection, fear, guilt, shame, lust, hatred, rage, murder and suicide were all present by this time. Some of this was inherited from her mother.

Rachel had conceived this son as she was being raped by her new husband, the son who ten years later would lead her by the hand to Eve and to me. As this terribly violent abuse was being perpetrated, a spirit of rage manifested through both of them. Out of this trauma, at the moment of conception, the son received the spirit of rage. This act of conceiving a child, which normally should be such a beautiful and wonderful experience, was a terribly traumatic experience for Rachel. From then on, sex could only bring back all of the terrifying events she had experienced, against her conscious permission and desire.

Demons certainly use trauma as a means of entrance. The evidence in this regard is overwhelming. Just as evident, however, are the results of the ripple effect. The demons remain and continue manifesting into succeeding generations, until they are eventually cast out by the power of the Holy Spirit in the name of Jesus of Nazareth.

THEIR STAY IS AIMED AT DESTRUCTION

The presence of a demon in one's life does not in itself bring about condemnation, but the continuing effects from its lingering presence weaken your resistance to temptation. The evil that emanates from the demon will, to some degree, change your character or personality from what it might have been had it not gained entry.

CHAPTER 2:

THE GREAT COMMISSION: DELIVERANCE

In the fourth chapter of the book of Genesis we read how Cain's face darkened and he became very angry. The Lord himself confronted him in his anger and told him that if he would only do what is right he would be accepted. God told him that sin was crouching at his door with a desire to possess him. But then came God's assurance. Following his warning, God told Cain that he could rule over sin if he would only do what is right.

Cain, like his mother Eve, was faced with a traumatic decision. He knew that God preferred blood as an offering **(Hebrews 11:4)**. It was easier to bring his own produce than to hunt up an animal or bargain for one with his brother. His heart was not right and God confronted him with a warning.

AUTHORITY IS YOURS

God commissioned Cain's father Adam to take dominion over all that lives in the earth **(Genesis 1:28)**. "All that lives" includes germs and demons. God then confirmed this to Cain, who was their firstborn. He warned him, first of all, that if he was to inherit the power given to his parents, he must be reverent and obedient. Cain demonstrated laxity in these areas.

Cain's trauma came through the predicament he faced. He could do things right or he could do them wrong. Wrong proved easier for him. His choice was so traumatizing that his countenance literally changed. The result brought about the entry of spirits of rebellion, jealousy, hatred and murder. These spirits had been around a lot longer than Cain, Abel or their parents, and they had waited a long time for a body to enter. Cain proved to be easy prey.

LAXITY IS DESTRUCTIVE

Proverbs 24:30-31 describes the vineyard of the slothful, lax or lazy man. The wall is broken down and overgrown with thorns and nettles. Isaiah 60:18 says to call the wall your salvation. Job had a hedge about him that Satan could not penetrate **(Job 1:10)**. You must do what is required to keep up and maintain this wall that *is* your salvation, or else thorns and nettles will keep you from producing the everlasting fruit that Jesus calls for from each one of us **(John 15:16)**. Thorns are the curse on fallen man, spoken upon him through Adam **(Genesis 3:18)**, and nettles are a poisonous thorn shrub. Luke 10:19 and Mark 16:17-18 give us power over poison. Snakes and scorpions represent spiritual poisons.

Jesus wore the crown of thorns to the grave. He now wears a crown of glory. We share with Him in His victory over the curse. Praise God!

A pastor of a fairly large church in a metropolitan area once asked us to see a young man he had just gotten released from jail into his custody. The man had been charged with indecent exposure and public drunkenness, and he also had a problem with drugs. Let's call him Art. After a bit of searching into his background, we learned that Art had experienced two traumatic experiences at an early age. While sitting in his father's car with his brother in their front yard, his father had come toward them from the house in a drunken frenzy, brandishing a gun and pointing it wildly at them.

His parents had sometimes left him and his brother in the custody of their female cousin. While baby sitting with them, she would openly expose herself and masturbate before them. This earlier traumatic experience, plus the later trauma caused by this incident of the gun, allowed the spirits of rejection, addiction and fear to begin controlling his life. The cousin's shameless activity had provided an open door for an unclean spirit. In time these spirits caused him to become a social misfit.

We showed Art the sources of his problems. We prayed with him and cast the spirits by name from his presence, in the name of Jesus Christ the Savior of mankind. With the help of the pastor and the church community, Art's way of life changed dramatically. We saw him annually for several years after our initial meeting. He became a born again, spirit filled Christian. He gained employment and overcame his social setbacks.

THE REACTION DETERMINES THE DAMAGE

During counseling, Art asked us a very interesting question. He asked why his brother was not affected as he was, when he experienced the same encounters we said were the beginning of Art's lifelong problems. My answer to him was that we each react to circumstances differently. His brother was not affected by those experiences in the same way that Art was. For Art they were traumatic, and for his brother they were not.

The definition of trauma is a disturbed or disordered state, resulting from a shock, injury, or wound. It is a mental or behavior-related condition brought on by a violent or shocking experience or encounter. It often has a lasting effect on people's lives. But, what was traumatic for Art was not traumatic for his brother. What shocked Art did not shock his brother, who accepted it more readily. They reacted differently to the same encounters. Art opened doors to certain spirits, while his brother either did not, or he possibly opened up to still different spirits, which would have caused his life to go in a different direction from Art's.

Trauma in itself is not damaging, it is simply a challenging or testing experience in life. The reaction one has to trauma determines the effect it can have on the years or even generations to follow. Trauma need not be damaging, but it quite often is. Trauma can be a doorway to a lifetime of sin, suffering and further trauma. And, most terribly, it can be the motivator to a life which will lead to eternal damnation.

Trauma occurs in everyone's life. It is part of life and cannot be completely prevented. It can be life threatening or it can be utilized to an advantage. The key is how you respond to it when it comes.

Trauma cannot always be anticipated. Unfortunately, the most damaging trauma often comes, as has already been pointed out, at such an early age or state of development that it is hard for the individual who might experience the harrowing experience to do much about it. This is one reason why it is so important for a life to be started as correctly as possible. You naturally cannot start your own life, so it is up to the parents to be prepared for childbirth.

It has been said that "an ounce of prevention is worth a pound of cure." This principal can be applied to the spiritual aspects of life as well as the natural. How a child is brought up has much to do with how it will develop **(Proverbs 22:6)**. How the child's birth is prepared for can also have great effect.

Parents who have established a strong, Word-based relationship, full of manifesting love, have great reason to anticipate a healthy child who will develop and grow into a good, God fearing person. Illegitimate childbirth, abuse and violence, as well as a lack of desire or attention toward the potential birth, are valid avenues for prenatal intrusion by various demons.

There is Scripture, as well as the previously mentioned evidence, which shows conclusively that the unborn child has a spirit and is very sensitive to what is going on in its immediate vicinity. All traumatic interferences involving the mother during her pregnancy are occasions which can develop into lifelong problems for the infant she will bear.

Saul, the first anointed king of Israel, was confronted with a traumatic decision. His life changed dramatically for the worse from that time on. The book of 1 Samuel tells how the man of God warned him not to lead his army out against the enemy until a sacrifice had been offered. Samuel was to perform the sacrifice, but not until he had returned. He said he would be gone for seven days **(1 Samuel 10:8)**.

When seven days had gone by and Samuel was nowhere to be seen, trauma came over Saul. Decision time. What do we do now? The enemy was before him **(1 Samuel 13:5)**. His people were fearfully departing. Some hid in caves, some followed him trembling, and others simply deserted him **(1 Samuel 13:6-8)**.

The spirits of rejection, rebellion, impatience and irreverence attacked Saul. He went forth and performed the sacrificial offering himself, which Samuel had made clear he was not to do. As soon as he completed the sacrifice, Samuel arrived and charged him with foolish disobedience **(1 Samuel 13:10-13)**. This wrongful decision by Saul, in a time of traumatic testing, brought a parade of spirits into his life. Spirits of torment, rage, jealousy, anger, hatred, murder, depression, confusion and suicide followed the original group of spirits.

THE QUESTION THAT GETS ANSWERS

A lady who has for many years opened her home on a weekly basis to prayer meetings arranged for us to counsel with a young spiritual daughter-disciple of hers. The woman was in her thirties at the time. As the session began, we quickly learned that the young lady was a lesbian. We will call her Wilma. We employed questions with prayer and a seeking of release of the gifts of the Holy Spirit, as we entered the deliverance session. We asked the question "try to recall your earliest recollections in life for us." This question almost always reveals occasions of early trauma in the lives of those we are counseling.

Now we realize that, under natural circumstances, there is room for a person to lie. There is also the interesting condition in which people seldom tell their true feelings, positions or attitudes initially. But that is in the natural, and in response to a direct question. We do not directly ask people to describe an early trauma. We ask for their earliest recollections. We are relying on the Holy Spirit and have joined them with us in prayer. We usually have also led them in a commitment or recommitment prayer. We have applied the blood of Jesus Christ and we have bound Satan, his darkness, wicked powers and evil spirits.

Wilma recalled an incident early in life when, as a very small child, she agreed with a little boy to expose herself to him as he exposed himself to her. Her mother scolded and shamed her for this. It was at that moment that the spirits of rejection and lesbianism entered into her and altered her life.

Rejection came because she felt her mother had rejected her. The lesbian spirit came because she totally misunderstood what her mother was telling her. Satan took advantage of the incident and confused her. With time, he even convinced her she was born a lesbian and could not change or be changed. She is now filled with the Holy Spirit and leads a very active life in Full Gospel Fellowship. Now there is nothing to keep her from moving into a healthy relationship with a man, which should lead to marriage. She just needs for God to bring the right man into her acquaintance. In the meantime she is very comfortable serving God as a single, delivered, heterosexual female.

We cast the spirit of lesbianism from a young girl several years prior to our meeting Wilma. This girl is living a totally delivered life today. She is happily married to a man and is very active as a born again, tongue talking, spirit filled Christian.

An interesting point to consider with Wilma is that her mother did not cause her to receive that lesbian spirit. Wilma's *misunderstanding* of what her mother was correcting her for doing is what opened the door to that life-changing spirit of evil.

UNITY VS. CONFUSION

We once had a woman accompany us when we went to pray for a woman with demonic problems. The Holy Spirit had already revealed several spirits through Eve and me, when the woman assisting us pulled out the book *Pigs in the Parlor*. She turned to the pages that document spirit groupings and began reading the names in sequential order. She asked the person we were counseling to tell us which spirits she had and which she did not have. I immediately stopped the counseling session and asked her to stop. I saw this procedure as dangerous. Since the devil is a liar, and he might have control of this woman's voice, I felt that we could not rely on the answers to the questions being asked.

I in no way am accusing this woman assisting us of being wrong in her tactics. I just did not feel they were properly pertinent to this case. We therefore did not have order, agreement or accord. Her tactics differed from ours. Trying to use both at once brings about division. This opens up new ways for the devil to capitalize upon. Our purpose is to minimize or eliminate his avenues of operation. We must get his demons out so the Holy Spirit can have more liberty in lives.

Wilma's mother's intent was to stop Wilma from doing things she should not do prior to being married. Wilma's impression of her mother's disciplinary action caused her to mistakenly believe that it was wrong for her ever to have sexual relations with a male. This inclination allowed the beginning of an influence which led her, over years of time, into a youth of fantasies. A spirit of lust and a spirit of imaginations took up residence and began developing Wilma's mind for the sinful life which was to follow. At age eighteen she entered into her first relationship with another female. She had affairs with several women before being set free by the power of God. One affair lasted for seven years.

And it all began with a traumatic misconception of a very correct and proper chastising from her mother. It may not have been as thorough as some might feel it could have been, but it was certainly correct. The fact is, demons are roaming about, seeking an opportunity to take a leech hold on lives **(1 Peter 5:8)**.

PREVENTION PREVENTS NEED FOR CURE

The best preventive medicine for something like this is for parents to be active in the spirit. They should pray and apply the Blood over their children constantly, even while they are still in the womb. They should observe their actions. They should bind Satan regularly from their lives and loose the Holy Spirit into their lives. They should encourage their children to pray openly, and they should listen to what their children are praying.

CHAPTER 3

BURDENS PRODUCE TRAUMA

The burden of responsibility brought considerable trauma in the life of Moses. He led the nation of Israel through the desert for forty years. Initially he was the sole mediator for all of their problems. Eventually the occasion arose for a spirit of frustration to move in. God told him to speak to a rock to receive water for the people and their animals. Instead of speaking, Moses struck the rock with his rod **(Numbers 20:7-11)**. He also pridefully took credit for the miracle **(Numbers 20:12)**. God eventually lessened the load by spreading his anointing onto 70 others. However, the sin committed by Moses kept him from entering the promised land **(Deuteronomy 34:4)**.

Although Moses had killed an Egyptian in his early life, the sin coming out of the traumas he experienced in the desert kept him from completing the assignment God called him to at the burning bush.

Diversion is a sly tactic used by demons. If you strain or stretch your attention on too many matters, or fail to devote enough time to prayer, praise, the Word and worship, they will move in on you. You should prepare to be traumatized. Sin, sickness, oppression or some other adversity will quite likely be the result.

The Apostles very wisely assigned some of their more worldly responsibilities, such as serving and distributing food, to deacons **(Acts 6:2-4)**. This did not hinder the spirituality of the deacons. Philip and Stephen, two of these deacons, both performed great spiritual acts in addition to their work assignments.

Giving high-priority time to God is essential to a well balanced life. Tithing includes time. God is entitled to at least 2.4 hours a day. Very few seem to give Him this.

Put God first and He will put you first. You cannot outgive Him. He says He will pour blessings out of the windows of heaven if you give Him what is His.

This will not eliminate trauma from your life, but it will enable you to cope with it with God by your side. He says He will not abandon or forsake you **(Joshua 1:5)**. He will not fail you **(Joshua 1:5 KJV)**.

REJECTION: OFTEN AN EARLY SPIRIT

Rejection is a very common spirit. It is found in most cases. It is very often the first spirit that people encounter. In fact, it is often met in the womb. It is also, in many cases, the dominant or strongman spirit **(Matthew 12:29)**.

David seems to have carried a spirit of rejection with him. Neither his father nor his brothers considered him for Samuel's anointing. Neither was he included in the family consecration in preparation for Samuel's service of sacrifice **(1 Samuel 16:5)**.

Even Samuel had to be warned by God from considering the outer or natural appearance of Jesse's older sons when choosing the candidate for the anointing God had sent him to Bethlehem to perform **(1 Samuel 16:1-11)**.

Rejection in David is evident when he meets his older brothers on the battlefield, where the Israeli army is faced with the daily challenges of Goliath the Giant **(1 Samuel 17:28-29)**.

Rejection in David's life became quite prevalent when he came into the company of Saul **(1 Samuel 18:9)**. He was criticized grossly by his wife Michal for dancing before the Lord **(2 Samuel 6:20)**. His son Absalom, along with Ahithophel, one of David's counselors, openly opposed him for his throne **(2 Samuel 15:12)**. Even on his death bed, Bathsheba, his queen, had to approach him with Nathan the prophet to inform him that Adonijah, another of his sons, was trying to steal his throne when he had promised it to Solomon **(1 Kings 1:1-30)**.

CHAPTER 4

SEVERING CONNECTIONS WITH GOD

Each of these events certainly involved trauma for David. Rejection for David, with Satan as the spiritual source, is logical and understandable. Jesus the Christ is well known to Satan. Jesus says He watched as Satan was cast from heaven to earth **(Luke 10:18)**.

The coming of the Messiah had been heralded and expected since the curse put upon Satan at the time of the expulsion of Adam and Eve from the Garden **(Gen. 3:15)**. Satan would block the fulfillment of God's word at every opportunity, if he could. And though he can't, he still tries.

If he could steal the throne from Solomon with Adonijah, he was all for it. If he could destroy David or his descending line to Christ, through Saul, Absalom or Adonijah, he would stop the fulfillment of God's predestined plan. Rejection was a dominant factor which he used for this purpose. That is why he uses it so formidably on so many like you and me, as well. And trauma is a major occasion he looks for to make his entry, through the spirit of rejection.

SIN IS DEATH

The wages of sin is death **(Romans 6:23)**. This terrifying declaration from God's word proclaims a very basic truth: with sin you die. God will not fellowship with sin **(Isaiah 59:2)**. There is no sin in His place of abode. You cannot enter with unforgiven sin.

This death is not the mortal death we all must experience, it is spiritual death. It is final death. It is the final and

25

everlasting separation from God, which John calls the second death **(Revelation 21:8)**.

The ultimate goal of every demon alive is to lead you to such a fate. Jesus Christ died that you might live. Demons live that you might die. They take advantage of every encounter that you have with trauma to try to drive another nail into your coffin of eternal death. The three nails of Calvary enable you to send their nails back at them!

DEATH: THE ULTIMATE TRAUMA

Death is nothing to fear. Death can be your victory. You can turn the ultimate trauma, the trauma of death, into your ultimate victory. Instead of accepting death as a fearful and traumatic experience, look at it for what it actually is, the miracle of miracles. It is the wondrous step to the resurrection.

Trauma in itself is not sin, any more than money is evil. The love of money is evil. So also trauma is simply an experience in life.

Neither is an attack from a demon or the presence of a demon a sin, anymore than temptation is sin. Sin is transgression of the law **(1 John 3:4)**. Sin must be committed. Temptation is merely a tactic of demons.

Submission to temptation is sin. Submission to a demon is sin. Willful retention of a demon is sin. Successful resistance to temptation or trauma is meritorious, heroic, admirable and noble.

Faith to overcome temptation is given through God's grace. It is also given to survive trauma without succumbing to a demonic attack. Sin is resisted with faith, and faith can be used to drive out a demon.

Temptation and demons, left to function unopposed, will win out. You will succumb and spiritual death, not heaven, will result. You must overcome. You must run the course. You must fight the good fight of faith **(1 Tim. 6:12)**. You must be prepared for the traumas as they come. Life is a test. Trauma is part of the test.

TRAUMA NATURALLY BREEDS FEAR

Trauma is part of the challenge of life. Trauma challenges you to set your course for the resurrection or else drown in the flood of demonic oppression.

The resurrection is your time for settling up. It is the time when God will repay you for all you have given Him. If your gifts involve the things of the world, the world will repay you. If you give what cannot be repaid by the world, you will be repaid by the One Who can. You will be repaid at the resurrection of the righteous **(Luke 14:12-14)**.

Jesus *is* the resurrection and the life **(John 11:25)**. If you follow Him, you will see the resurrection and live forever. You will see Jesus. And He will not let you stand stripped, He will garb you in Himself. He will clothe you in His righteousness and in the light of the resurrection, His light.

So if you have fallen, from some of your traumas, to the attacks of invading demons who took advantage of your moments of vulnerability, you need not fear. Remember, Jesus fell three times trying to get to the top of a hill on your account. He died on a cross and was buried in another man's grave that you might have hope in the resurrection. There was no need of a grave of His own. He had no intention of remaining in it. Hallelujah!

DO NOT FEAR GOD'S POWER

So, you are told not to fear. You are told hundreds of times not to fear what you can't see. God is the God who tells you not to fear Him or His miracles. Each time His Word says "fear not" in the King James translation He is preparing you for an encounter with His wonder-working ways. He is getting ready to do something supernatural. He is getting ready to unfold a miracle before you. This is not something to fear, it is something to embrace.

On the other hand, each time He confronts a demon, the demon is the loser. He tells *you* to make them losers as well. He gives you power to trample on them **(Luke 10:10)**. He tells you to cast them out **(Mark 16:17-18)**. He tells you to resist them and they will flee **(James 4:17)**.

The Word tells you over and over not to fear. Do not fear demons. Do not fear sin. Neither should you fear the power of God. It is for you. It is for your children. It is for all whom the Lord our God will call **(Acts 2:39)**. It is your power over fear, demons and sin.

Two sisters and their brother attended a revival with us in a small church in a small town. They came for several nights. The pastor knew many of the townspeople who came but he knew nothing about these three teenagers. The middle aged child was a girl. She appeared to be unable to talk. She held one arm across her body, and her lips had some sort of a twitch to them.

I went to where she was seated and tried to get her to talk. The younger brother told me she could not. I began looking her straight in the eyes and I started telling her over and over that Jesus loves her. A large wide smile came on her face. The older sister said that had not happened before, that her sister had never smiled before.

I felt led to talk to them about showing forgiveness and kindness to each other. The boy sort of cowered and withdrew from me. The girl who couldn't speak became very sullen. Their response to the move of the Spirit ceased.

Being in the midst of a powerful move of God in a packed out church, I moved on to others. People were being saved, healed, delivered and filled with the Holy Spirit, so I did not get back to those three children that night.

The next night the oldest girl came forward. She accepted Christ and manifested deliverance rather profoundly, before the entire congregation. Then she received the Baptism in the Holy Spirit. She told me that they were victims of parental abuse and abandonment. She did not say it, but I felt impressed of the Spirit that they were victims of incest as well.

She told me that she had acted as mother to the other two. They apparently were living alone without adults. I then counseled with her to begin pouring the love she had received there that night, out upon the younger two. I encouraged her to minister kindness and compassion to them. I was trusting for God to complete the work He had begun through her. I felt then and I still believe today that the only way to reach those two younger ones was through their older sister. These kids had experienced terrible trauma. Their only contact with rationality and good sense had to come through her.

God planted his Spirit in that underage substitute mother that night. I'm confident He will use her to drive the spirits of rejection, fear and rebellion from that young boy, as well as the spirits of dumbness, torment, fear and paralysis out of the little girl. With any cooperation at all, He is going to heal them as He did her of the lasting effects of the trauma they obviously received through the heinous acts of their parents. The severed relations, caused by demons, between ourselves and God, as well as others, can and must be repaired. Deliverance is part of that restoration.

CHAPTER 5

HOLINESS --VITAL TO COPING

INCEST, A NESTING PLACE FOR SATAN

The nineteenth chapter of Genesis portrays a graphic example of how the trauma from incest can lead to rippling conditions which may continue to torture victims for generations to come. The eighteenth chapter of Leviticus forbids sexual relations with all close relatives, including parents with children and children with parents.

After God's removal of Lot and his wife and daughters from Sodom, and the loss of his wife, Lot took up residence in a cave with his two virgin daughters. They got him drunk on wine and had sexual relations with him as he slept. Their reasoning was that there were no other men around and that it was the only way to continue the family line **(Genesis 19:32)**.

Lot was one who chose the natural over the spiritual **(Genesis 13:10-11)**. He chose to live among homosexuals because the neighborhood looked good. He got himself captured and ensnared by the enemy, simply because he was associated with Sodomites **(Genesis 14:12)**. He was a poor witness, unable to convince his sons in law of their impending doom **(Genesis 19:14)**. He was a procrastinator, arguing with the Lord when told to flee immediately from his home **(Genesis 19:18-21)**. He had a disobedient wife **(Genesis 19:26)**. So it is rather questionable as to how valuable the family line of Lot really was.

Regardless, these unnatural and traumatically sinful acts of Lot's two daughters, following all of the trauma they had previously encountered, resulted in the births of Moab and Ammi, whose descendants remain the enemies of Israel today. They are still bringing traumatic havoc on the nation after these thousands of years, because the daughters of Lot made their wrongful decisions in the light of their traumatic plight.

Trauma can bring about many reactions. Lot stood at his door with two strangers in his home. The Sodomites of his chosen town were threatening to break the door in and take the men to be used for their sexual pleasures. Lot reacted to the trauma by offering his virgin daughters to them for the men's safety. Consider Lot's home as your mind. Regard his door as your senses. Now, look at the pressing Sodomites as demons.

YOU CAN'T BARGAIN WITH SATAN

Trauma has come to your home. It has opened the way to demons. They are trying to get into your mind. Their pressing is through your senses. Dilemma has arrived. What do you do?

Don't ever do what Lot did. He tried to bargain with them. You can't listen to a demon. He is a liar. The only power he has is the power you give him. He receives his power by getting you to listen. He gains entry through your sensual yielding.

CAST YOUR CARES ON THE LORD

The Lord shows you what to do through His experience with Lot. Let Him handle it. Put Him in charge. He will fight for you **(Exodus 14:14)**. Let Him do it. Either turn it over to Him or yield your total being to His indwelling power. The battle is His, says the Lord **(1 Samuel 17:47)**. But, for Him to take over, you must *will* Him to do so. God will *never* supersede your will. He wants you His, but He wants you free!

TRAUMA FROM WORDS

We met a young man in his late twenties. We will call him Bill. He lived with his mother and father, having never been

31

married. Upon leading him back to recollections of his early years, he related two experiences of trauma. He told us how his father, who was apparently joking with Bill, chided him because he was underweight. He said on numerous occasions, "Boy, you're so skinny your shorts are gonna fall off!"

This accusation proved to be true trauma for little Bill. He began clutching his undershorts when he would stand. By the time he reached school age he was not only clutching his shorts but he was pulling them up. Eventually he had them several inches above his pants. This trauma brought on the spirit of rejection.

The other trauma occurred when he witnessed a terrible accident. A young person died violently before his eyes. This brought the spirit of fear and the fear of dying. Then came the spirit of schizophrenia. As he retreated from one personality to another, his father rejected him further by ridiculing him. The kids at school had a field day with him. The spirits convinced him his nose was too big. He believed his hair was ugly and that there was no place for him in society.

The first time we prayed with Bill we cast all of the spirits out of him. However, as he was walking back home the devil came back at him as Jesus tells us he does **(Matthew 12:43-45)**. Trauma reoccurred as Bill had difficulty finding his true self. Within a matter of days the spirits returned.

We have seen Bill on several occasions over a period of several years. We have seen him strengthen and then regress. His father and his home seem to be a continuing obstacle to his complete healing. On one occasion we explained to him how these spirits were persons and how they manifest their own personality through him. He gave each one of them a name.

After naming at least eight persons who were cohabiting with him, he asked if he could step outside for a few minutes. As he was opening the door to leave he looked back and said "When I come back I'll tell you about one that is really something." When he returned, he said, "My heart has beat within me for thirty-two years. Not once has it beat for me. I would like to live for me. I would like to go to a Burger King without having to hide under a newspaper. I would like to be able to have a wife and children." Then he named four or five more spirits.

Bill reads several chapters of the Bible daily and he prays fervently. On several occasions he has interpreted an utterance of tongues from an adjoining room. He seldom is able to sit through a service with a congregation. Unfortunately, his life is one of constant and continuing trauma. These spirits have gained such dominant control in his life that his life is a trauma in itself. We are still praying for Bill at this time. We are trusting that God will provide a way for him to be free of not only the influences within himself but also those that are in his daily presence, which have him imprisoned as a sort of stranger within himself. The Lord sent the legion of demons from the Gadarene into a herd of pigs and then sent him off to another town to preach the wonders and the glory of God **(Mark 5:19)**. I feel that this scripture provides the key to Bill's healing. Hopefully it will come soon. I believe it will come when Bill musters enough boldness to overcome the fear which restrains him from gaining his freedom.

YOU CAN'T OUTGIVE GOD

Ridicule is a terrible form of persecution. Hannah, the mother of Samuel, suffered great ridicule from her husband's second wife. 1 Samuel 1:1-28 relates the story. One wife had borne the husband sons and daughters, but Hannah's womb was barren. Still, Hannah's husband loved her greatly. Knowing she was loved was not enough. This woman's constant badgering caused trauma so great that Hannah could not eat. It went on for years. She found her deliverance through prayer. She prayed so fervently out of her heart that no literal words came forth, even though her lips were moving.

Eli the old fat priest thought she was drunk. This reminds us of the occasion of Pentecost, which Peter says fulfilled the promise of the Father **(Joel 2:28-29)**. Those preferring to remain carnal accused the 120 of Acts 2:13 of being drunk. They were impressed only by what they could see in the natural.

A WALK IN THE LORD IS
A WALK IN STRENGTH

1 Samuel 3:1 tells us that there was very little manifestation of the Spirit in the life of Eli. His sons were so contaminated that they stole the offerings to God to fill their own bellies.

Jesus tells us to ask, seek and knock **(Matthew 7:7)**. Peter says we should grow in the spirit **(2 Peter 3:18 Ampl.)**. Paul says to pray and even to sing in the spirit, as well as with understanding **(1 Corinthians 14:15)**. Jude tells us to build ourselves up in our holy faith by praying in the Holy Ghost **(Jude 20)**.

Living in the spirit strengthens our commitment and reinforces our resolve. Yielding to the Spirit instills greater resistance to Satan. Allowing the Holy Spirit to manifest His gifts through us enables us to overcome the enemy. Isaiah 10:27 (KJV) says the anointing breaks the yoke.

You can put your spiritual need on the altar of God by speaking it out in everyday language. This is asking. You can then seek your need by praying in the Spirit. Romans 8:27 says our utterances are heard by the Father, as the Holy Spirit groans or appeals for our need. From there you can knock, you can break through into the very throne room of God by moving fully into the Spirit. Trauma and the evil spirits it opens you up to hinder and obstruct this three-step process of prayer. This is why it is so vital that you use the gifts of supernatural abilities God has given you to respond spiritually to these attacks.

RAPE, A FAVORITE TRAUMA FOR SATAN

We were asked to see a young woman in her thirties several years ago. When prompted to recall early events in her life, she said she remembered nothing before age 21. The event she recalled was rape. I'm sure there was much of her youth and childhood she could have remembered, but the Holy Spirit was in charge. Time was short and He brought the incident to her mind.

The trauma of this terrifying abuse to her body opened the way for the spirits of fear and insecurity. Afraid that she would become promiscuous, she soon married. However, this brought more trauma. The traumatic memories, coupled with the antics of the demons, prevented her from entering into normal relations with her husband and he beat her and raped her until she finally divorced him.

LINGERING CONSEQUENCES

The next husband was a pastor who had problems of his own. He had spirits of pornography and fantasy. This marriage went the same way. Eventually she divorced him, but not before getting him to burn all of his pornography.

The third marriage lasted only a few weeks. She left after the first beating. She is completely healed today and will make a fine Spirit-filled wife, as soon as the Lord sends her a good Christian man. In fact, at this time, he may already be on the scene. Time will tell.

These people who experience these terrible traumas need more than deliverance, they need healing as well. That ripple effect needs to be stopped. Even after the healing, they need continued counseling, prayer, advice and reassurance. This lady has called us from several states away on numerous occasions. She is still sending in good reports.

CHAPTER 6

THE MIND AND THE WILL

YOU'VE GOT TO FIGHT TO WIN

Romans 7 reflects the circumstances of spiritual battle that are there for each of us. Paul tells how the Law or the Word of God reveals to us the perils of sin. If it were not for the Word, we would not even know what sin is or how to resist or overcome it.

He explains how the commandments of the Law identify sin and prohibit you from yielding to sin's temptation. He uses himself as an example for all. He was born not knowing the Law. Then he learned about right and wrong from the Law. The conflict between his inner self and his flesh kept him in constant trauma. This trauma tended to bring him under Satan's domination **(Romans 7:7-12)**.

It is not the holiness of the Word or its righteousness that brings you into condemnation. It is the awareness of your state of separation from God, which the righteousness of God's Word produces, that convicts you of your condition. This in itself is intended by God to break your spirit and bring contriteness **(Psalm 51:17)**. It is a healthy reaction to trauma. It is by God's saving grace that we are saved and raised into heavenly realms with Christ Jesus **(Ephesians 2:5-6)**.

Paul goes on in Romans, the seventh chapter, to emphasize the continuance of the battle of the spirit and the flesh. He explains how your natural sinful nature joins with sin itself to overcome your spiritual desire to do good. You want to do what is good but you just keep right on doing what is evil. Since you are doing what you do not really want to be doing, Paul concludes that it is not really you doing it. It is the demon he calls "sin dwelling within you" who has taken over a part of your life. It has gained such a hold on you it is causing you to act against your will and the will of God. His conclusion is that your only hope is to call upon Jesus Christ to rescue you **(Romans 7:25)**. This is what salvation is all about. It is also what deliverance is all about.

You are fighting a losing battle. You are fighting an unseen foe. You are fighting an enemy which, in many instances, you don't even know is present. It is an enemy which most people refuse to admit even exists!

I am a native Miamian. I grew up in the subtropics of South Florida. I was eighteen years old before I saw snow. I first observed it from the deck of a ship while viewing the mountains of Portugal.

Eve was born in Northeast Mississippi. We have lived in both parts of the country. The first time her parents came to visit us in the winter in Miami, the first words out of her father's mouth as I welcomed him to our home was, "Paul everything here is green." He was greatly impressed with the fact that the trees do not shed their leaves in the winter, as they do in less temperate areas. Before the day was over, he remarked to Eve that he was finding my homeland to be "like a paradise."

Now suppose for a moment that my first trip North had been at the same time of year in which he had traveled South. Assume that I had never seen trees shed their leaves in the Fall. Even though I had heard about it, I refused to believe it because I had never seen it. Let us suppose, now, that I am seeing what I believe to be dead trees and foliage everywhere I look. Everyone tries to assure me that they will come back to life again, come Spring, but I just go back to my paradise, refusing to believe that these trees could be resurrected back to life.

This is the position so many people take regarding demon spirits, miracles, healing and, in many cases, hell, heaven and life after death. Acts 23:8 tells us that the Sadducees did not believe in the resurrection of the dead. Neither did they believe in angels or spirits. The Pharisees believed in it all. Both groups, however, were tied up in a maze of man-made traditions. Jesus says that the traditions of men nullify and void the Word of God (Mark 7:13).

There are, it would seem, many Pharisees and Sadducees still walking around. Everyone has an opinion. There are many, however, who have had true spiritual experiences with angels, demons and manifested miracles, healings and utterances given by the Holy Spirit. Some can even tell you of an experience with death, of a visit to heaven or hell, and of having seen Jesus Christ, Himself. An experience supersedes an opinion every time.

God substantiates His Word with manifestations. Mark 16:17-18 says that signs will follow or accompany those who believe. Believers are to cast out demons, speak in new tongues, have no fear of snakes or poison, and they are to lay hands on the sick, that they might recover. All of this is to be done in the Name of Jesus by those who believe in Him.

Believers are to expect supernatural acts from God in their lives. It is a major facet of the Christian life. Experiences in the spirit are a normal and natural part of being a Christian. They are God's way of showing to those who truly believe, the firstfruits or a foretaste of the glory which He has in store for us through the resurrection of our bodies from the grave (Romans 8:23).

Expecting experiences that can only be related and not fully explained is part of being a believing Christian.

ALL THINGS ARE YOURS TO DO

Jesus had told the father of the demon-possessed son that all things are possible to those that believe (Mark 9:23). The disciples marveled at His taking authority over nature, saying, "What manner of man is this that even the winds and the sea obey Him?" Nature would have obeyed them, had they stood against it in His name. It will obey you if you stand against it in 'His Name'. Paul says you can do all things through Christ Jesus. He says it is Jesus who strengthens you **(Philippians 4:13)**.

God told Adam and Eve to subdue the earth **(Genesis 1:28)**. As their descendants, we have inherited their curses. But, as we become part of the 'Family of God', we inherit the blessings of Abraham **(Galatians 3:29)**. We are co-heirs with Jesus Christ **(Romans 8:17)**. He has been given all power in heaven and in earth **(Matthew 28:18)**. Authority over sickness, demons and even the elements is yours as an anointed, spirit-filled son of God. All you need to do is exercise it.

REACTING DIFFERENTLY TO TRAUMA

Trauma could have been experienced by Joseph when he learned that Mary was pregnant. He could have put her away **(Matthew 1:19-20)**. Instead he welcomed an angel and the message that he brought, rather than the demon who was obviously trying to tempt him. Trauma is a way into the soulish realm. You can, however, go either way.

GREATER IS HE WHO IS IN YOU...

As Jesus came down from the mountain where He was transfigured, He had Peter, James and John with him **(Mark 9:2)**. When they joined the other disciples, they found them arguing with those teachers of the Law who were always ready and willing to espouse their opinions to the point of argument.

The disciples of Jesus who had not gone with Him up the mountain had tried to cast a spirit out of a man's son. They had not succeeded and a tumult had followed. The man told Jesus that the spirit would seize his son, throw him to the ground or into fire or water, and that it had stricken his son with dumbness and even tried to kill him. All of this is found in Mark 9:1-29.

The man accused the disciples of not being able to drive out the spirit. He then asked Jesus if He could do anything to help in this traumatic situation. Jesus proceeded to tell him something that is later recounted in Mark 16:17-18. He said everything "is possible for him who believes." The father answered, "I do believe." Jesus then drove out the spirit for all to see, as the spirit shrieked, caused the boy to convulse violently, and finally left.

Those who had been skeptical earlier, witnessed something they could not deny. They saw the Spirit of God take charge over an evil spirit. They saw the evil spirit resist and they saw it desist. They saw victory in Jesus.

Later the disciples questioned Jesus about why they were unsuccessful with this demon. The nineteenth verse of the chapter finds Jesus saying earlier, "Oh faithless generation" or "Oh you bunch of unbelievers." These words still speak to the opinionated of today. He is not speaking to the disciples as individuals. They believed. They had seen spirits cast out, and had even cast them out themselves. He is speaking to the disciples in general, as well as to a generation of unbelievers, which includes these present days in which we live. He is speaking to the latter-day generation, which lacks the faith to use the faith they have been given. He is also speaking specifically to the admitted unbelief of the father of the boy with the demonic problems.

He spelled out a condition to the father. He told him his son could be delivered, if he would believe. All things are possible for those who believe **(Mark 9:23)**.

FAITH IS THE KEY

The father admitted he was an unbeliever. He said, "help my unbelief." But he also said the key words, "I do believe." When he said those words, the key turned in the lock. The boy

40

was set free. Faith is what it takes—released faith—spoken faith, actuated faith, prayerful faith: MOUNTAIN MOVING FAITH.

Faith is the power that operates the universe. Faith comes only from the throne of God. Faith is ours to have and use in exchange for an expressed will to believe.

CHAPTER 7

YOUR VISION IS YOUR MINISTRY

TRAUMA AN OPPORTUNITY FOR VISION

Faith is the needed implement for you to use to convert trauma into vision instead of disaster. When trauma comes, demons come. They come to take advantage of your moment of panic. They have every intention of entering your life, with the sole purpose of destroying it.

Your deterrent to their attempt is vision. Vision will enable you to establish and maintain a reason for making order out of chaos. Vision presents aims and goals in a time of confusion.

THE STORM ON THE LAKE

Matthew, Mark and Luke all tell of Jesus calming a storm in the midst of a lake. Jesus got into the boat and the disciples followed Him. Their destination was the other side of the lake **(Matthew 8:18, Mark 4:35, Luke 8:22)**.

The King James version of Luke's gospel says they "launched forth." They headed out in obedience, for a specific goal, "the other side." They knew where they were to go and they were making an effort to get there.

Suddenly their voyage was interrupted. A great storm came down upon them, the boat was all but swamped, and they found themselves in great peril, about to sink into the depths of the lake. Their trip was about to end in disaster. It did not appear that their destination was to be reached. Trauma was confronting them from all directions.

THEY LAUNCHED FORTH

The disciples knew where they were to go, but they did not know why. They had a goal, but they did not have a purpose or a reason, and yet they launched forth! They went on until trauma came upon them.

HIS CALL IS YOUR VISION

Jesus gave them their commission. He issued a command. He gave them a vision. They were on a mission. They were to row the boat over to the other side. With that, He went to sleep in the boat, leaving them in charge of reaching their destiny or destination.

HEAD FOR YOUR VISION

Jesus has given you a commission. You are under orders. You have a vision. You are told by the Word of God to launch forth. You are commanded to head out into the world. You have been ordered to carry the good news to the world.

Jesus *is* the Good News. Jesus *is* the Gospel. Jesus *is* the Word (John 1:1). He was in the boat with the disciples. He was asleep, but He was with them as they proceeded toward their vision. They had a vision, planted in their minds by His command to reach the other side. They were in His service. They were ministering to Him by attempting to comply with His commission.

Confident that His command had been clear and explicit, Jesus went to sleep. He was relying on them to complete their act of ministry. They knew where to go and they knew how to get there. They were proficient at rowing a boat, and so He went to sleep!

Jesus has given you a commission. He wants you to launch forth. He wants you to be a witness for Him (Acts 1:4). He wants you to believe in Him and, as a believer, He wants you to speak in tongues, cast out demons and heal the sick ((**Mark**

43

16:17-18). He wants you to receive the baptism in His Holy Spirit **(Acts 1:5)** and He wants you to exercise authority over the powers of the enemy **(Luke 10:19)**. This is your ministry. This is your vision!

HE HAS NOT LEFT YOU TO THE STORM

In the case of the disciples in the boat, he lay down and went to sleep. In your case He has ascended into heaven and seated Himself at the right side of the Father **(Revelation 3:21)**. In both circumstances a vision has been established. A ministry has been launched.

He has put a task in your hands, just as He did with the disciples. You have something to do for the Master and you have the authority and the power with which to do it. That's vision. That's ministry.

NO VISION, NO HOPE

The author of Proverbs says that, without a vision, you will perish **(Proverbs 29:18)**. Isaiah says that, if you refuse to serve, you will perish **(Isaiah 60:12)**. He includes all of the nations and kingdoms of the world in this declaration. He sees them launching forth, with ships bringing sons from afar, loaded with silver and gold. They are destined for the wide-open gates of the dwelling place of the Holy One of Israel. They are coming to minister to Him. They are coming to build up His walls **(Isaiah 60:8-11)**.

In the eighteenth verse Isaiah says to call your walls "salvation." Here is your vision. Here is your ministry. Here is your service to the Master. Build up the walls of your salvation. Paul says to work out your salvation in fear and in trembling **(Philippians 2:12)**. This is to be done while Jesus sleeps, or reigns from His throne above. It is to be done by you in fulfillment of the vision He has given you. That vision is all you need to carry you through the storm of life. That vision is adequate for you to complete your ministry. It is ample for you to build your wall of fulfilled salvation. It is all you need to get to the other side. However, you can expect storms of trauma to rise up in opposition as you launch forth.

THERE'S A STORM WITH EVERY VISION

As the disciples were rowing the boat, attempting to fulfill their Christ-given vision, they encountered one of these life threatening obstacles. A great storm arose, which threatened the continued existence of their ministry. A mountain suddenly appeared between them and their destination. Trauma was standing between them and their vision.

Having a vision is not sufficient in itself for its fulfillment. If your vision is the realization of the call God has put on your life, you can count on a storm. Satan will surely bring something against you as soon as you launch forth. Set your course and Satan will throw all of His power at you. He will do all he can to discourage or deter you from staying true to your vision, and trauma will be the occasion he will anxiously await.

All three gospels reveal the reason for the storm when they tell why Jesus wanted to reach the other side of the lake. In a place called Gadara, on the opposite shore, lived a man tormented by a legion of demons.

The vision was not complete for the disciples—it seldom is. Your ministry is a ministry of faith. As you walk in the light, you come into greater light. John calls it a fellowship light, which cleanses you from sin as you walk **(1 John 1:7)**. As the light cleanses you, darkness leaves and you continue coming into a greater fullness of the understandings God wants you to enjoy. This is the process of continuing deliverance or progressive sanctification.

However, your first steps must be faith steps. Your vision walk begins from where you are. You must launch forth, trusting God to guide you and use you by His Holy Spirit, to

His full pleasure. Go where He leads you and He will use you as you go.

As you launch forth, anticipate deliverance. It will come just as surely as it did for the disciples in the boat. Satan knew that Jesus was sending them into one of his own strongholds. Gadara not only had a man running among the graves and screaming through the night in utter torment, but it had a population of traditionalists who did not want to change.

Once, as Eve and I prepared to leave a church in which we had experienced a successful weekend of ministry, Satan tried to take advantage of trauma with us. As we left for our next assignment for the Lord, we heard a loud noise from behind. We pull a thirty-foot trailer from place to place in our ministry. I stopped and went behind the truck, where the trailer connects. The heavy steel clamp that holds the leveling bars had snapped. It had broken off. The bar was lying in the street.

I had noticed for some time how the bars were bent like a bow when connected but, not knowing how they were supposed to look, I had done nothing about it. I took a coat hanger and tied the bar up so we could move. We were in West Memphis, Arkansas. Just a few blocks away we found a mobile home repair shop. It was early morning, cold and misting rain.

The man behind the counter came outside with a replacement clamp. He took one look and said that his clamp was different from mine and it would not work. He said, "See, my clamp is different from your broken clamp," as he held one beside the other. Then he told me that if we would cross the river to Memphis, there was a trailer hitch place on Summer Avenue that could fix it. As we were crossing the Mississippi River bridge to Memphis, it began to rain hard. It was Monday morning, with rush hour traffic building up fast.

On North Parkway, as we headed for Summer Avenue my windshield wiper blade on the driver's side popped off and lay before us on the hood. We were in the center lane of traffic with two lanes between us and the curb. Unable to see clearly, this certainly was a time of trauma, with full occasion for panic to occur.

That was when I realized that we were under attack. I immediately spoke loudly and commanded Satan to take his hands off God's property and leave. In some way that can only be attributed to the grace and glory of God, I managed to change lanes and pull into a service station. I picked up the windshield wiper blade from atop the hood where it had remained and popped it back into place. By the time we reached the trailer hitch shop the rain had ceased.

The man there came out with the correct clamp, took one look at ours and said, "Mister, your clamp is not broken, there's nothing wrong with it." I stared down in utter amazement at that rusty old clamp, restored by God to its original, prebroken condition.

Before I could praise the Lord, the man said, "What you need is to replace those leveling bars. The load you're pulling is too heavy for the size you have. If you don't change them, you could have a bad accident. We had it done and drove off into a clear day, giving praise and glory to the Lord.

Satan did everything he could to get us to panic in that time of trauma, but we pressed through. We took authority and overcame the crisis by the Lord's great hand. God used the incident when we remained calm and allowed Him to show us the way through the storm to bring us safely through the crisis.

Satan tries to protect his strongholds with an armada of traumatizing scare tactics. He used a storm against the disciples and was quite successful. The storm was a "mountain," deployed to keep them from reaching their vision of the day. The vision of the disciples was that far shore. On the shore, the man with some 2000 demons was awaiting their arrival. Satan tried to stop them with the storm and the disciples countered by crying out to the Master. Jesus arose, exercised authority over the elements and commanded the storm to cease. Then, according to Luke, He asked them, "Where is your faith?" **(Luke 8:24)** Mark says He charged them with having "no faith" **(Mark 4:40)**. Matthew describes them as having "little faith" **(Matthew 8:26)**.

ARE YOU USING YOUR FAITH?

Paul says that everyone has been given a measure of faith **(Romans 12:3)**. So, they *had* faith. Jesus challenged them with not using what faith they did have. What little faith they had was used to call out to Him to save them, lest they perish **(Matthew 8:25)**.

He is saying, "Where is your faith? How is it that you have no faith, oh you of such little faith?" He is asking them why they called on Him. Why didn't they just use what they had been given? How is it that their faith was hidden and not displayed, when it could and should have been? Why didn't they use the little bit of faith it had taken to call on Him and use that faith to calm the storm themselves?

SUCCESS IS THERE BEFORE YOU START

When Jesus issues an order, it is a command to ministry, and with it comes the vision of its success. When He told them to go to the other shore, nothing could have stopped the fulfillment of that vision. Satan could not have stopped them, neither could the world or the natural elements of the earth. Nothing can stand against the Word of God.

When they reached the other side, Jesus set the possessed man free. The legion of demons left him and entered the herd of pigs. This is an example of the Word going forth under the supernatural power of the Holy Spirit. When you speak the Word with the authority you have been given, something has to happen. The Word will not return void. It goes forth to accomplish its end. It carries with it a vision or purpose as it is spoken **(Isaiah 55:11)**.

After being delivered, the man came to Jesus full of vision. He wanted to follow Him wherever He went. There was no more desperate need. This man was ready. He was full. His deliverance did not leave him dry **(Matthew 12:43)**. His vision was his ministry. His vision was his testimony.

Seeing this, Jesus sent him out immediately. He told him to go and tell others of the great things God had done for him **(Mark 5:19)**. When your vision comes, it's time to launch forth in ministry. The man began the fulfillment of his ministry by sharing the wonders of God's mercy and miraculous powers at Decapolis, which means Ten Towns. His vision began to be realized as he went from town to town, telling the good news **(Mark 5:20)**. His vision was to witness the wondrous works God was now doing through His Son, Christ Jesus. And all men marveled at what they saw and heard **(Mark 5:20)**.

For the townspeople of Gadara a different story unfolded. When the man was set free, word spread rapidly through the town and the surrounding countryside. When they came out to see what had happened, they saw the man who had been possessed, sitting clothed and in his right mind **(Mark 5:14-15)**.

They had the same opportunity to catch hold of the vision as those of Decapolis. Gadara, however, was a stronghold of Satan. Here was another mountain. Instead of marveling at the signs and wonders performed in their town, they allowed fear to enter in **(Mark 5:15)**. They rebuked the vision. They refused to accept the ministry of Jesus. They told Him to depart from them. They told Him to leave their shores, and He did **(Mark 5:17)**!

Here you can see an example set forth from four sectors. The man set free of the legion of demons was immediately filled with vision, power and ministry, and those he witnessed to marvelled at his testimony. The people of Gadara refused the vision. The apostles had to continue on in the vision for more first-hand training. All of them responded in different ways to the trauma they encountered.

We each respond differently to visions as well. When Pentecost came, the 120 spoke in tongues, ministered in anointed boldness and reeled under the power as if they were drunk. Three thousand were added and baptized on that same day. Many others refused the vision **(Acts 2:13)**. The trauma resulting from this great and wonderful spiritual phenomenon was just too much for many to handle.

Philip had such vision that, even though he had been given a title of deacon and a position of responsibility to wait tables, he still launched forth in a ministry of great power, signs and wonders **(Acts 8:5-8)**.

Having vision, as discussed so far, means looking into the potentialities. It is seeing things before they become reality. It is the capacity for imagining things that can be sought, achieved, obtained or done. It is developing the potential that lies in dreams, revelations or oracles from God into plans for future accomplishments.

A vision, as described by Ezekiel, John the Revelator and many others, is the literal seeing of invisible subjects, just as though they were visible. It is the beholding of things from the spirit realm. It is the experience of looking upon the countenance of spiritual things, using the capacities of your spirit's ability to view things and to register them in your mind, whether they are seen by you in their outward form or not.

Moses saw the Angel of the Lord as a burning bush. God appeared to Abraham as three men. Ezekiel saw a rainbow-draped throne and dazzling multi-winged creatures with wheels within wheels beneath them. This is not necessarily the vision which translates into ministry.

You may or may not see a vision as you envision yourself successfully serving God in a certain way for a certain purpose, with a certain goal as your prophetic perception. Vision in this sense is an impulse or realization that offers the proposal, opportunity or compulsion to seek out a worthy goal which God has imposed on your heart.

Vision, as mentioned in 1 Samuel 3:1, is the "ministry" type of vision. There was not much foresight or true ministry to be found in Eli and his sons. The King James says it was precious, which means rare. They were bound up in self and, as Proverbs 29:18 declares, they accordingly perished. He and his two sons met violent deaths **(1 Samuel 4:17-18)**.

The type of vision which enables one to see invisible things could not have been strong with them, either. With sin in their lives and the lacking of any visionary ministry, there certainly was not much place for a supernatural move of God in the way of visions, prophecy, miracles and healing.

The interesting aspect of this is how God will raise up a standard in the midst of such debauchery. With the sins of Eli and his sons blocking visions and vision, the young boy Samuel, placed under Eli's care by his mother, ministered before the Lord **(1 Samuel 3:1)**. The mother had given him to the Lord as a climactic part of his miraculous birth. This generous act of true *agape* love undoubtedly brought forth vision in young Samuel's heart.

Under these circumstances the Lord appeared to Samuel. He heard Him call him three separate times during the night. The third time He actually stood before Samuel **(1 Samuel 3:4-10)**. In Samuel's vision he saw the Lord standing before him. He received vision from the Lord when he was told Eli's future **(1 Samuel 3:11-14)**. His vision, as a ministry, was planted in his heart and increased with time as he grew up with the Lord always near him. Samuel never let the Lord's words fall to the ground **(1 Samuel:3:19)**. As a result, Samuel became a great prophet for Israel.

Vision, then, births ministry. It begins with an envisioned goal. This would generally presage or foretell any manifested action. Usually the vision, or perceived opportunity to serve, will lead you into an actual service, which could include many more visions. The vision to serve comes by faith, as does the service itself. You don't need much. Matthew speaks of "little" faith five times in the New International Version. There of course is the occasion spoken of in the storm on the lake **(Matthew 8:26)**.

When Jesus spoke to the multitude, He showed how God provides for all of nature, in order to challenge those of little faith to rely on God **(Matthew 6:30)**. He charged Peter with using little faith, when He had to rescue him as he began sinking from his walk in faith on the water **(Matthew 14:31)**. Peter certainly was fulfilling vision as he stepped from the boat into that stormy sea. He faltered out of fear, as trauma opened the way to doubt. As he looked about himself at the threats posed in the "natural," the trauma blocked out his visionary confidence. He forgot his vision of following Jesus when he allowed the flesh to subdue his spirit, as he reacted to the impulse put forth in his mind by the spirit of fear.

HIS CALL IS YOUR VISION

Jesus and His call on your life must be your constant vision. It must be nurtured in your heart, retained in your mind and pursued in your flesh. You must live out your vision day by day. It must be the primary priority of your life. It must be your overcoming deterrent to trauma.

Jesus accused the disciples of having little faith when He showed them how the yeast of the Pharisees can poison the spiritual food of the Word **(Matthew 16:8)**. In Mark 7:13 He warns against the traditions of men. They nullify the effectiveness of the Word.

Deuteronomy 8:3 compares natural bread to spiritual bread. The Word of God is food to your spirit and soul. Spiritual nourishment must have first priority in your life. The "traditions of men," which includes legalism and carnality, are birthed by religious spirits. They have close kinship with controlling spirits and spirits of witchcraft and idolatry, which

Samuel says bring about rebellion and stubbornness against God's ways **(1 Samuel 15:22-23)**.

Jesus also accuses the disciples of having little faith on the occasion of casting a demon out of the young man whose father had asked Jesus to have mercy on his son **(Matthew 17:14-21)**. Having little faith is not bad at all, if you actually *use* it. The total amount of faith is not pertinent, the utilization of it is. Jesus says it just takes a little faith to move an entire mountain **(Matthew 17:20, 21:21)**. "Mountains," in this sense, are seats of spiritual resistance. They are the deterrents to the realization of vision. They hinder ministry service. They are obstacles to reaching and achieving your spiritual goals. The solution is expended faith, regardless of the quantity.

FAITH MINISTERS

The lack of faith kept Jesus from ministering successfully in His home town of Nazareth **(Matthew 13:58),** so He dusted His feet as He tells us to do **(Matthew 10:14)**. He left Nazareth and made Capernaum His hometown **(Matthew 4:13)**. He found enough faith there to heal the paralytic and forgive his sins, but He still encountered resistance. The legalists accused Him of blasphemy **(Matthew 9:2-3)**. He later cursed that city, along with several others, for not repenting when they saw the miracles **(Matthew 11:20-24)**. Miracles are for repentance. They are true ministry.

DEMONS ALSO EXPERIENCE TRAUMA

So here we have seen obvious obstacles to successful ministry. Unbelief, and failure to receive or respond to the works of God nullify His workings. In Mark 7:13 Jesus attributes this to "the traditions of men." Walking with a vision will always bring the culprits out into the open. They are your opponents and you can count on them to come crawling out from under their rocks when you come into their territory.

Your anointing brings about trauma for them. They react traumatically to the blood of Jesus, as well as to the anointing of the Holy Spirit.

As soon as Jesus forgave the man of his sins, the teachers of the law came on the scene, accusing Him of blasphemy **(Matthew 9:3)**. That old accusing spirit, spoken of in Revelation 12:10 raised up his head in opposition. The releasing of God's power, however, puts him to flight. The crowd was filled with awe when the paralytic they all knew picked up his mat and went home **(Matthew 9:6-8)**. So, hold to your vision, perform your ministry, use the power given you and watch the devil cower with trauma as observers marvel in true conviction. There will always be opponents, but there will also always be those who will respond.

GREAT FAITH

Jesus marveled at the great faith He found in the woman who argued with Him for the children's bread **(Matthew 15:28)** and in the centurion who recognized and respected His authority **(Matthew 8:10)**. Neither of these were Israelites.

The woman was arguing for deliverance for her demon-possessed daughter. Jesus referred to this as bread reserved for Hebrew tables, since that was where He was sent **(Matthew 15:24-26)**. He contended that it should not be wasted on gentiles, whom he compared to dogs. This potential trauma was overcome as she stood her ground.

She countered by saying that even dogs eat crumbs of bread when they fall from their master's table. Here she indirectly calls Him Master. She pursues her vision of deliverance for her daughter. She tactfully ministers to Him on her daughter's behalf and she succeeds as He grants her petition and compliments her for her great faith **(Matthew 15:28)**.

The centurion receives the same grant and compliment for his bold acknowledgment of His authority to heal. He believed so strongly that he asked Jesus to heal his servant by a long distance dispatch of His healing virtue. He challenged Jesus to heal his servant without knowing his name, seeing him, or even being in the servant's vicinity. He asked Jesus just to "say the word." There is no limit to the power of the Word. Distance has no weakening effect. Jesus marveled at this expression of faith aimed at the realization of the centurion's vision of healing for his servant.

Jesus told the woman who touched the hem of His garment that her faith had healed her. Her bold pursuit of her vision propelled her confidently through the trauma of having to press through the crowds, encouraged by her conviction that touch alone would heal her. It worked!

Matthew 9:29 says two blind men were healed in direct accordance to their faith. They used it and they were healed accordingly. They said they believed that He could do it and they spoke with conviction. That's all it took. Their vision of sight for their blind eyes was realized.

TURNING FROM THE FAITH

Paul refers to the latter days as days in which many will turn away from the faith. Millions today call themselves Christians while fulfilling this terrifying prophesy. They deny the power in the Gospel **(2 Timothy 3:5)**. They refuse the faith as a means of manifesting God's power among men. They refuse the vision of miracles and healing as ministry for today.

CHAPTER 8

FAITH: GOD'S POWER IN ACTION

The definition of faith includes two words, according to *Strong's Concordance*. These words are "conviction" and "reliance." Faith cannot be separated from the spiritual power of the Holy Spirit. It is through faith that you are saved **(Ephesians 2:8)**. Your exercising of the faith measured out to you by the grace of God enables the Holy Spirit to literally create a new reborn spirit within you **(Romans 8:11)**. This is an exercise in supernatural power on your part, as well as on God's part. So, expended faith is the utilization of God's spiritual power. It is miraculous power, which has been experienced by every born again believer!

Faith is the evidence that proves there is substance to the unseen spiritual realms. Faith is the substance that enables you to enter those realms and use the power that comes only from those realms, to achieve things both mortal and immortal, which you might hope for **(Hebrews 11:1)**. This is power beyond your own natural capacities. This is God's very own power within you. It is poured into you as you are filled with His Spirit.

If you do not use this power by utilizing the God given faith within you, then it dies, out of separation. James says that if you separate your faith from works, your faith is dead, in that it is alone **(James 2:17)**. The spiritual definition of death is separation from God. Faith is your spiritual link with God. When you refuse to use your faith for supernatural purposes, you break your link of faith with God. Your faith is dead. It is alone. You are alone. You are dead.

CONVICTED TO RELIANCE

Faith screams for you to become convicted to reliance on God's supernatural Holy Spirit power. Faith screams for you to live in the spirit. Faith screams for you to walk and work in the spirit. Faith screams for you to grow in the spirit. Paul says that you may have power together with all the saints to the measure of the fullness of God **(Ephesians 3:18-19)**. Unlimited usage of God's power to His fullness is yours for the asking.

The disciples launched forth, headed for the other side, without full understanding as to why they were going. That's faith in action. However, they went without total conviction or reliance. They headed for the other side still stuck, to some degree, in the lingering, legalistic, carnal traditions of men. They went still carrying fear. They went forgetting to use the faith in which they were being instructed by the One sleeping in their midst. They went susceptible to the consequences of trauma.

Their failure to use the faith God had invested in them left them exposed to the perils of nature. They used only a little faith, they cried out to the Master for Him to do what they themselves could have done. Had any one of them stood and done what Jesus did, they would have reached the other side just as safely as they did by calling on Him to get them through the storm.

Not only could they have calmed the storm, they could have cast the legion of demons out of the man on the other side. They had the power by His calling. They found this out later, when He sent them forth on their own to cast out demons and to heal every disease and sickness **(Matthew 10:1)**. The name of Jesus carries that much power!

A woman, let's call her Annie, was referred to us. Annie, we discovered early in our initial counseling session, suffered from controlling and tormenting demonic voices, as well as actual physical abuse from demonic forces. She had been married four times and had an eleven year old son from still another relationship. She lived in public, low-income housing and was in a rehabilitation program, which provided secular counseling and employment.

She had been sexually molested as a small child by uncles, brothers and even her mother. Her father abused her physically and she suffered from verbal abuse and abandonment.

We actually observed invisible forces beating her on her arms, body and neck as we spoke to her. Bruise marks appeared on her skin from these spirit attacks, as we watched. We had considerable success in the initial session. Annie reported a few days later that her production at work had improved, thus increasing her confidence and her income.

We managed to explain to her how blood on the doorpost protected the Israelites at the time of the exodus out of Egypt. We then translated that point to her own body. By laying her own hand on herself, she sealed her doors against continued intrusion.

We showed her how her senses are the entranceways to her inner self. By symbolically applying the Blood of Jesus, abuse was greatly curtailed. She even took a broom and symbolically swept the evil forces out the door of her home, loudly commanding them to leave her natural residence as well. She did this, of course in the Name of Jesus. Immediately thereafter she said she felt and saw dark clouds leaving her body by way of her mouth.

After several sessions, the beatings stopped, but the voices remained. She was attending a church that apparently was more concerned with her meeting their legalistic requirements than helping her with her problems. They had laid a burden of guilt upon her because her hair had been cut.

She asked questions such as, "Will the Holy Spirit tell me to do bad things? Will the devil ever tell me to do good things?" She was troubled by religious spirits and spirits of guilt. They had her greatly confused about what is right and what is wrong in the eyes of God.

As I was explaining to her that the Holy Spirit will never lead you into evil, but that the devil plays both sides of the fence, I felt impressed to ask her a question. I reminded her how the sin of Achan had kept the Israelites from victory when they first attacked the city of Ai **(Joshua 7:19-20)**. Then I asked her what she was hiding. What was she holding back? I said, "There has to be something that is keeping us from breaking through to victory."

She then confessed her retained guilt concerning her mother's violent death. I pressed for the circumstances. It was obvious that she had no justification for carrying the guilt. I then managed to convince her that she should let go of all of her feelings of guilt. We got rid of those spirits and more progress was made.

In our next conversation she told me a neighbor had invited her to a revival at her neighbor's church. The pastor told of trips he had made to Africa and how he had discerned and cast out demons while there. He called her out of the congregation and cast still more demons from her.

She told me that this helped greatly. She felt free of the demons that had oppressed her for so long, but she said she had a "dead feeling" inside of herself. I explained to her how Jesus said cast-out demons will return and check you out to see if you are still empty **(Matthew 12:44)**. I made the point that the emptiness needs to be replaced and filled with the Holy Spirit. With that, the conversation ceased.

Within minutes the phone rang again. It was Annie, reporting that she felt alive and full. She excitedly proclaimed that she was singing and praising the Lord. She said that she had not been that happy nor had she praised the Lord like that for a great number of years.

Annie was free of the torment and torture that had held her in bondage for most of her entire life. Trauma in her early life led to continuing trauma throughout her life, which opened many doors for Satan to punish her, to what would appear to be quite nearly the limit of endurance to which God allows us to be tempted **(1 Corinthians 10:13)**. A part of her never gave in. A part of her never quit holding out for survival, and God honored her desire and perseverance.

Today Annie continues to fight her battle. Step by step she is learning to put those tormentors on the run. She asked Eve just recently if she thought she would ever be really free. Her secular counselor has told her, just as they tell alcoholics, that she is sick and will never get well. She has been told to admit daily to a continuing condition of illness. When Eve told her she was free and that she did not need to allow those oppressing demons back into her life, ever, she screamed with elation. Joy welled up in her with the assurance that she could be free in Jesus. She expressed the new joy in her heart.

Annie carries her Bible with her to work. She witnesses to her fellow workers and shares her testimony as she rejoices in the peace she says she has found through the expulsion of those demons who had tormented and beaten her for so many years. Jesus says that if you are set free, you are free indeed **(John 8:36)**! Nahum 1:9 says that affliction shall not rise again. The Word of God does not lie. Annie is free and Annie is happy in her new life in Christ Jesus.

People who converse with the devil are going to lose. He is a liar and a tormenter. He is too sly for the natural mind. Annie was a prime example. It took weeks for us to get her to stop listening to demon voices and to praise the Lord instead. Next, she learned to begin ignoring them. Only then were we able to prepare and condition her to hear the voice of the Lord.

THE MAKEUP OF MINISTRY

The calling of Christ is clear in the sense that He wants you to do the same things that He did. As a believer He wants you to walk with a vision. He expects you to launch forth in conviction and reliance. He wants you to use your God given faith by taking authority over the enemy. He wants you to witness, through the ministry to which He has called you.

Paul describes ministry as fivefold. He says there are apostles, prophets, evangelists, pastors and teachers **(Ephesians 4:11)**. This is vision. To perceive yourself in one of these categories and to seek out the accomplishments He has for you to reach, is the realization of ministerial vision.

The purpose of such vision is explained by the apostle Paul. You are called into ministry to prepare God's people to serve. Service is ministry. So vision for ministry is for everyone. We are to bring this message of ministry to one another. This message is the solution to the threat Satan poses through trauma.

God's people are to be prepared by those in the fivefold ministry to serve, so that the Body of Christ will be built up. God wants growth in His body. He plants a vision in each of us to participate in this calling.

Unity in faith, knowledge and maturity in the fullness of Christ is the actual vision. This is the goal. This is the reason you are called to Christ. You are called to grow in His love, into a vibrant, living organism, tightly knit in mature, singular faith, power, knowledge and understanding of the things He would have you know and do in conformance with His Word.

> It was He who gave some to be apostles, some to be prophets, some to be evangelists, and some to be pastors and teachers, to prepare God's people for works of service, so that the body of Christ may be built up until we all reach unity in the faith and in the knowledge of the Son of God and become mature, attaining to the whole measure of the fullness of Christ. **(Ephesians 4:11-13)**

The job each and every one of us is called to is to save souls, feed the hungry, set captives free, shore up the flock and arm the unarmed. You are to be about the Father's business. You should constantly be striving in the power of the Holy Spirit to help in the building and development of a strong, loving, healthy body of mature souls, knit closely together in love and strength, in worship and service to Almighty God. Nothing should hold you back from this commitment.

Until you encounter that storm of opposition, you have not yet fully set your course. You have not yet launched forth. Trauma will most certainly continue to be used by Satan as a distraction and a deterrent. There is much he can and will use to keep you from reaching the other side. If you are really committed, count on an attempt at entry with every trauma.

THE OPPOSITION

There are basically four categories of opposition you face. The disciples faced all four as they launched forth: (1) They could have failed to get into the boat, (2) they could have failed to row the boat with enough perseverance and (3) failed to row in the right direction to reach their goal. Finally, (4) they could have given up and turned back when they encountered the traumatic storm.

There are an uncountable number of reasons for not getting started. You have got to answer the call. Even Moses had excuses for not going. Jeremiah said he was too young. The Gadarenes refused the call outright, whereas the one that had been delivered of Legion was anxious to serve.

Complacency and laxity will cause you to rot. The author of Proverbs says he looked at the lazy man's wall. It was falling down in ill repair and the grape vines were choked with thorns and nettles **(Proverbs 24:30-31)**. You must strive to lift yourself above the traumas of the world's ensnarements of conformity and carnality.

There must be direction. You must have vision, reason and purpose. The trauma of double-mindedness will leave you rudderless **(James 1:6-8)**. You'll never reach that heavenly shore if you don't daily set your life in that direction.

There is no place for frustration, confusion, distraction and outright backsliding! You must face the traumas head on and press for the mark **(Philippians 3:14)**. It is a good fight, a fight of faith. God is on your side. He will fight for you. He will fill you up with His Holy Spirit. He will garb you in His full armor **(Ephesians 6:11)** and He will lead you through the storm. He will bring you through every trauma you face. The success of life is found in three steps: they are decision, commitment, and follow-through.

Life cannot be lived without trauma. Neither can it be successfully lived without vision. Your vision must become your ministry. Ministry cannot function without faith, and faith is dead without power. Unless you live a life in the supernatural service of Almighty God, the tools He gives you to live it with will perish from you. They will leave you just as Jesus left the Gadarenes when they told Him to leave them alone **(Mark 5:17)**!

God poured out His Spirit upon all flesh on the day of Pentecost. He is still pouring out that latter rain **(Joel 2:28-29)**. It is yours to have and to use. It has no other purpose than to immerse you in the fullness of faith, hope, love, power, wisdom and understanding. It is poured out to bring forth lasting fruit in your life **(John 15:4)**. Trauma is a major obstacle to your immersion in these wonderful aids to living life in the abundant spiritual fullness God has provided for you. Experience the vision of Pentecost. Launch forth in the spirit. Use the gifts of the Holy Spirit freely and constantly in your life and trauma will become simply a passing opportunity to gather the testimony that will make you an overcomer over the Accuser of the Brethren **(Revelation 12:10-11)**. You will have locked the door of trauma which he has used to gain entry to where he might bring death and destruction to the lives of so many millions.

CHAPTER 9

LOOK BEYOND YOUR TRAUMA

Peter encountered trauma as he walked on the water. He began to fear the storm as he walked because he took his eyes off Jesus **(Matthew 14:30)**. He cried out to Jesus to save him.

Paul and Silas faced trauma in jail. They praised the Lord and the chains fell off. The jailer and his household were saved while experiencing trauma. The jailer was so traumatized he was preparing to commit suicide **(Acts 16:27)**.

Judas faced trauma as he realized how wrong he had been. The very one who could have saved him is the one he betrayed. Even so he could have still turned contritely back to Christ, and Jesus in all his love and compassion would have forgiven him and cast those spirits of rebellion, guilt and suicide from him.

CARNALITY HINDERS FAITH

Martha was frustrated in the trauma of trying to prepare a meal for the Lord while her sister sat at His feet and listened to His words. He reprimanded her and she went back to her kitchen with His blessings. She lived in the natural but she still loved the Lord.

Later with the trauma of having lost her brother Lazarus she tried to cope with the mystery of the resurrection as Jesus told her He is the resurrection and the life. He told her whoever believes in Him and lives will never die. He asked her if she believed this. She answered him that she did believe. She believed that he is the Christ, the son of God—the promised one, the Messiah **(John 11:21-27)**.

Martha still did not fully understand. But she went and told her sister that Jesus had come to them **(John 11:28)**. When Jesus told them to roll back the stone from the tomb of Lazarus it was still Martha who objected. Her carnality was still fighting the truth as it stood right in her face. All she could consider was the reality of her brother's death. He had been in the grave now for four days, and a terrible odor had undoubtedly developed **(John 11:29-39)**. But still she remained, still she obeyed.

Her cooperation turned her trauma to joy. Jesus prayed to the father that those like Martha who have difficulty believing in the supernatural power of God might see. Jesus called Lazarus out from the tomb.

Lazarus was undeniably dead, yet Jesus gave him back his life. Jesus restored his mortal body and restored him back within it. This occurred not only before the eyes of Martha but of his disciples and many other Jews as well.

These people were good religious people, no different from so many of today. They were comfortable serving God in their own way, but to serve God in His way was just too much. Many are deluded by false light. 2 Corinthians 11:14-15 says that Satan is not only able to change himself into an angel of light, but his servants or ministers are able to change themselves into ministers of righteousness.

Their biggest lie is built around carnality. Don't get in too deep, they will say. Stay rational. Follow your intellect. Keep away from the irrational. Don't have anything to do with things you can't see. Follow these skeptics and you will fall for Satan's most skillful delusion.

PRAYER—A HEALTHY REACTION

Jesus himself experienced unbelievable trauma as He prayed in the garden of Gethsemane. The anguish was so terrifying that great drops of blood poured from the glands of

His skin **(Luke 22:44)**. He was so weak that an angel had to come and strengthen Him **(Luke 22:43)**.

He realized what was in store for Him. His hour was at hand. The hour God had promised mankind from Adam had arrived. The hour He knew He would encounter from before time began was near—the hour man had awaited for generations. That hour was unfolding. Satan realized what was really happening. He would have tried to stop its fulfillment if he could. However, it was the hour of hours. It was the hour of man's redemption. It was the hour Jesus understood fully. It was the hour in which He would take upon Himself all of the sin, affliction and adversity of the entire human race. Jesus was experiencing trauma in one of its most extreme forms, and it had nothing to do with His own physical suffering. It had to do with the "God part" of Him touching and tasting sin.

It was more than He in His flesh could bear. The traumatic struggle had to go well beyond the scope of the natural. He finally had to ask that it be taken from him if at all possible. He gave it over to the heavenly realm. He yielded it to the will of the Father **(Luke 22:42)**.

Three times He prayed **(Matthew 26:44)**. Three times He found His disciples asleep when He had asked them to stay awake. They were overcome with sorrow **(Luke 22:45)**. His trauma was beyond their endurance. Their flesh could not sustain this terrifying hour. A great high point in the battle of all battles had arrived.

TRAUMA WEAKENS YOU

These are battles to be fought in the spirit. They can not be won in the flesh. Jesus tried to warn His disciples of this. He asked them to watch with Him. He asked them to watch and pray for one hour **(Matthew 26:40)**. He explained to Peter that they were to watch and pray so that they would not fall into temptation. Trauma weakens your mental, physical and even spiritual resistance. Jesus pointed out that the spirit can be willing but it can be hindered by the weakness of the body **(Matthew 26:41)**. This results in a weakened spirit. This scripture shows how failure to watch and pray can cause you to slip into temptation. Temptation comes with trauma. It is a way into sin. A sinful state results from yielding to demonic influence. Demons are constantly watching for the opportunity to bring you down into their estate **(Jude 6)**.

STAY ALERT

Jesus is telling you, as He tells the disciples, to watch for these demons. He was not telling them to watch for the soldiers He knew were coming. He was telling them to look with Him, and He was looking much deeper than down the road on which the soldiers were approaching.

SIN IS TRAUMA

Neither was He fearful of the mortal death He knew was about to occur. His great trauma-causing anguish was over what the imminent death was all about. Sin is what it is all about.

Sin is the most abhorrent thing that God confronts. Sin is totally repugnant to everything God is or represents. God wants no part of sin. He has hated it since its occurrence through the prideful rebellion of Satan.

JESUS IS THE ANSWER

Jesus the God-Man—Jesus the man sired by God himself—Jesus the son of God is the One whom God the Father had looked to for the removal of the stench of sin from His nostrils, once and forever more. Jesus was sweating blood. This hour He was asking for from His disciples was heralding the climactic hour of the deliverance of man from the traumatic clutches of sin.

THE HOUR OF HOURS

Jesus was going to have to immerse Himself in sin to get us out of it. He was going to have to immerse Himself in every sin, sickness, disease, loss, injury and grief that had occurred or would ever occur. He had to climb that hill called Calvary. He had to make it into the altar of altars. He had to mount that cross of crucifixion. He had to desecrate Himself with the most terrible defilement man has ever encountered. It was just a matter of hours from the hour of total defilement. He was just hours from the hour when He would take upon Himself the entire defilement of all men from all past and future times.

TRAUMA—A TIME OF TESTING

Trauma does not in itself cause demon entry. It is not an occasion of sin. It is not an instrument of temptation. Trauma is an experience. It is an experience that occurs in the mind. Trauma is a mental reaction to a shocking encounter.

Trauma is a time of challenge. It is a time of testing. The results and the effects of trauma are determined in the mind. What develops out of trauma is determined by how it is reacted upon.

Isaiah 48:10 says that we are chosen from the testing or refining in the furnace of affliction. Trauma is an instrument of affliction. Trauma is the mental testing which accompanies the anguish of suffering. Trauma is the furnace God uses to observe your reaction as well as your progress as you experience the sufferings and affliction which occur as you go through the melting pot of life.

Are you going to place yourself freely upon the potter's wheel for working or reworking? Are you going to be a willing lump of clay in His hands? Or are you going to stubbornly and rebelliously shape your own life? This is how God is observing you. He gives you total freedom to do as you will. But He lets you know that His way, the way of yielding to His spirit by your spirit, is the way into the comforts and joy of His everlasting bosom.

We once received a phone call from a man requesting prayer. As Eve and I prayed, she received a word from the Lord for the man. She wrote it down. I received a vision which I drew as best I could. The picture looked like a very large-mouthed fish with large eyes. The view was from the front and the mouth was wide open. It was sucking a flame into its mouth.

I mailed the word and the drawing to the man. He called back saying he understood the word provided through Eve. He said that it fit him and ministered to him, but he didn't understand the drawing.

A few days later he called again. He had been browsing through a used bookstore where he bought an out-of-print book containing scenes from old movies. In it he found a picture from an old black-and-white movie in which the star was posing as a prostitute standing in the midst of an African voodoo ritual. Just to her side was a war shield. On the shield was painted the grotesque fish I had drawn for him from the vision. It differed only in that its mouth was full of long, sharp teeth, and the flames were not present.

The narrative in the book suggested that the figure was a demonic god named *Vagina Dentata*. I had never heard of this demon, nor had I ever seen a picture of it prior to the vision. The narrative described the god as being in the form of a shark. I prayed about it and an explanation unfolded for the man. He had suffered as a child from a controlling and domineering mother with an alcohol problem. He grew up with problems of procrastination, guilt and an incompleteness in his attitude toward women. He had experienced three unsuccessful marriages and other attempts at relationships had proven unsuccessful. He also had a lot of rage and violence in his life.

The Lord then had me tell him that the prostituting action of the demon had actually sucked his fire from him. It had stolen his ability to function fully and freely in seeking and giving love. It had sucked away a lot of his capacity for reaching spiritual fullness as a Christian, and it kept him in an unstable state of spiritual flux.

This revelation, along with Eve's word, served to accelerate the work God had been doing in him during the two years prior to this act of spiritual impetus. With this revelation his eyes were opened wider to the call God has on his heart.

THE WEAKNESS OF
THE FLESH VS. SPIRITUAL POWER

The spirit must overcome the flesh. As trauma comes the weakness of the flesh will lead you into temptation, sin and demonic ensnarement. The spirit will lead you to God and His overcoming wisdom, power and love.

THE CERTAINTY OF PROPHECY

Isaiah 48 in its fullness calls you to listen to the Word of the Lord. It tells you the things of the past and shows the fulfillment of His prophetic revelations. It tells you of what is to come and gives you His absolute assurance that, just as the earlier things he foretold occurred, so also the things of the future will just as certainly come about. It reveals His love for us and it uncovers the hidden mysteries of His wonderful and spiritual ways. It offers you irrevocable righteous citizenship in the everlasting Holy City of the almighty creator of the universe. And it assures you that He is big enough, good enough, and cares enough to bring you through the tribulations and testings that you must pass through on your journey with Him into His eternal habitation.

Hebrews 12:5-6 challenges you to remind yourself of the exhortations of encouragement which come from the Word of the One who addresses us as sons. Do not take lightly the rebukes and chastening disciplines which bring pain and hurt into your life. But rest assured that these frustrating and oftentimes lengthy sufferings are simply part of the chastising learning process we must sustain as children of God.

The challenge in this testing is to overcome the flesh side of man which is weak, and which on its own will succumb to these traumas. The successful passing through of these painful experiences in life demands patient perseverance, which can only be accomplished with the strength that comes from the spirit and not from the flesh.

DELIVERANCE IS YOURS TO HAVE

> As for you, because of the blood of my covenant with you, I will free your prisoners from the waterless pit. Return to your fortress, O prisoners of hope; even now I announce that I will restore twice as much to you. I will bend Judah as I bend my bow and fill it with Ephraim. I will rouse your sons, O Zion, against your sons, O Greece, and make you like a warrior's sword.

(Zechariah 9:11-13)

These verses from Zechariah shed more light in this area. Rather than succumb to the pangs of traumatic anguish, be enlightened and enheartened by the covenant you have with God. It is a covenant made in blood. It is made with undefiled, not contaminated, blood. It is made with the blood of the perfect Lamb. It is a covenant given to us with the blood of Jesus. Because of this blood the prisoners of the waterless pit can be freed. This is God's covenant with man, cut in stone through Moses and in blood through Jesus. God's testament with man states that you do not need to remain in the pit which has no water. You cannot live in the natural without water. It is a basic condition to survival. Water in the Bible represents the Holy Spirit. God is emphatically associating His Holy Spirit with basic spiritual survival.

The pit is Satan's prison **(Revelation 20:7)**. The Psalmist and the author of Proverbs both say that if a man digs a pit for himself he will fall into it. **(Psalms 7:15, Proverbs 26:27)**. Isaiah refers to the pit of corruption and destruction as a place of soulish confinement **(Isaiah 38:17)**. He accuses the dealers in woe and treachery of ensnaring the inhabitants of the earth into fear and the pit **(Isaiah 24:16-17)**. Proverbs 23:27 identifies a pit with a whore, a prostitute or a strange woman.

The prostitute of Revelation 18 is the great religious spirit which seduces man into her haunts of filth and unclean spiritual adulteries. It portrays one who reigns as a queen but who keeps you from abiding spiritually in the Spirit and Truth of almighty God. So the pit is the world and it's evil and dry ways.

Zechariah says God wants to deliver you. He wants to set you free. He wants to bring you out of the dryness of the world and its ways. He wants to save you from the dryness of man's doctrines and traditions. He wants to release you from the ignorance you have toward God's Word. This ignorance impoverishes you spiritually.

He wants to heal the brokenhearted, bring deliverance to the captives, recover sight for the blind and set free the bruised or oppressed **(Luke 4:18)**. This is a proclamation of Jesus from the scroll of Isaiah the Prophet **(Luke 4:17)**. It is the ministry of Jesus. It is the ministry of deliverance of mankind from the waterless pit. It is the work of the Holy Spirit. It is the flooding of goodness from the throne of God into the heart of mankind.

When you succumb to temptation, when you play with sin, when you go your own way, when you panic from the traumas which occur in life, you dig yourself a dry well you can't get out of. You continue to struggle in your plight but your struggle is in vain. The more you strive in these ways of man the deeper you get in this dried-up well.

Your only way out is to call out to God for help. When you call to Him as your heavenly Father, Jesus tells you in Luke 11:11-13 that, just as an earthly father would not give his son a snake or a scorpion when he asks for food, neither will your heavenly Father refuse you the Holy Spirit if you ask for Him.

CHAPTER 10

DELIVERANCE—TRUE HOPE

IMMERSED IN THE HOLY SPIRIT

The baptism in the Holy Spirit is an artesian inundation of the flooding flowing waters of Ezekiel 47, Revelation 22:1 and John 7:38. It is a spring of living waters from which you will never thirst **(John 4:14)**. It is the baptism spoken of by John the Baptist in all four gospels when he said he baptized in water but one would come after him and baptize with fire. It is the promise of the Father **(Acts 1:4)**, which Jesus says you must have in order to witness in power **(Acts 1:8)**. It is the baptism that fills you with the New Testament power of God **(John 14:17)**. It makes you more than the Old Testament prophet who had the Holy Spirit with him—the anointing power upon him. You become the Ark, the Tabernacle, the very Temple of the Holy Spirit. The presence of God actually takes up residence within you!

Zechariah 9:11-13 continues to say that, as you are freed from that dry pit of hopelessness, you are to turn to the stronghold. You are called to turn to your fortress. God's offer to take you out of the pit includes a call to strength. His call is your hope. Turn to Jesus. Turn from the hopelessness of the world to the hope of Jesus. Turn to Him for the rendering of a double portion.

PASSING THE MANTLE

Change from your ways of entanglement. Repent to God's ways of empowerment. You will receive the anointing that was upon Moses, Joshua, Elijah and Elisha. It will be passed on to you, just as it was passed on to Elisha **(2 Kings 2:9-12)**. Elisha asked for a double anointing. He asked to receive, as to a first born, the passing on of what the father has to give to the eldest son, for an inheritance. This was significantly fulfilled as Elisha, seeing the ascension of Elijah, cried out "Father, Father!" He picked up the mantle, parted the Jordan and went forth to perform twice as many miracles as his predecessor **(2 Kings 2:13)**. This is exactly what Jesus says we are to do **(John 14:12)**. The Spirit of Elijah went to Elisha. It went to John the Baptist **(Luke 1:17)**. It filled Jesus, the hundred-and-twenty at Pentecost, and still fills every born-again, Spirit-filled believer who asks to follow in that power.

Zechariah continues on to proclaim that the Lord will bend Judah as a bow. He will fill it with Ephraim. He will make you like a mighty warrior's sword. This New-Testament baptizing in power unites you with God as an all powerful entity which Satan, his demons and the world's forces of darkness cannot prevail against **(Matthew 16:18)**.

A study of Deuteronomy 33 and Genesis 49 reveals the exciting aspects of this union. These are the scriptures which, in Genesis, describe the blessings given by Jacob to his sons and in Deuteronomy by Moses to the twelve tribes of Israel.

It began with Abraham, who received the covenant from God. Abraham passed it with a blessing to Isaac, his first born by marriage. It did not go to Ishmael, born of Sarah's maid **(Genesis 21:12)**. Isaac then passed it on, through the laying on of hands, to Jacob. Jacob was not the first born, but his older twin Esau did not appreciate his heritage and he traded it for a bowl of soup **(Genesis 25:30)**. Jacob passed it on to all of his sons as well as the two sons of Joseph **(Genesis 48:5, Genesis 49)**.

God's preference of Isaac over Ishmael demonstrates the necessity of staying in God's will, hearing His Word and trusting Him to fulfill it. Jacob's being favored over Esau shows that the things of the Lord are invaluable. The granting of them, however, requires responsibility and accountability.

With Jacob we see increase or expansion. The anointing was then expanded to the entire family of the first born. As time reached the third generation of God's chosen people, this family of just over seventy was led into Egypt because of famine in the land.

We now observe the occasion of mass traumas. Within 400 years the family grew into a nation enslaved in the land which originally afforded sanctuary to them. So the cry from Goshen—the cry of trauma, the cry of affliction—went forth from the furnace of Egypt to the ears of the Lord **(Exodus 3:7)**.

God sent Moses to deliver this nation, His anointed, out of the world—out of Egypt. He brought them miraculously into the wilderness, where He changed the conditions for anointing **(Numbers 13:6-8)**.

As His plan of salvation continued to develop, further increase was manifested. He looked now for a closer relationship among the masses. He therefore changed the procedure of anointing the firstborn to anointing one of the twelve tribes. The Levites became the anointed priestly intermediaries between the Israelites and God. They were taken out of secular society and empowered to minister service and atonement to God.

All of this points to the continuance of perfection as we go from glory to glory in His plan, which is bringing us into His likeness in Christ Jesus **(2 Corinthians 3:18)**. This includes the step taken at Pentecost in fulfillment of Joel 2:28-29. His anointing is now for all flesh.

As the patriarch Jacob laid his hands on his own sons and then on the two sons of Joseph, Jacob invoked special spiritual identities and abilities upon them by the words he spoke. Moses did the same as he invoked his blessings upon the tribes of Israel on the occasion of his parting from them just prior to their crossing over the Jordan into the promised land. These identities and abilities became the traits of the inheritance they were to pass down to their descendants.

THE BOW AND THE ARROW

The special anointed abilities of Judah and Ephraim are found in these two invocations. Judah is a young lion. He is the defender against the foe. He is a ruler and a leader. He has permanent power. He operates with stealth and cunning. He has authority over the world. He is tied to the vine, and he is established as the choicest branch.

Jesus is from the tribe of Judah. He is known as the Lion of Judah **(Revelation 5:5)**. Jesus is certainly our defense against the foe. Proverbs 30:5 says that every word of God is pure. He is our shield if we put our trust in Him. Jesus is our defender. Submit to Him and the enemy must flee **(James 4:17)**. He is the King of kings **(Revelation 17:14)**. He has authority in heaven and earth **(Matthew 28:18)**. He is the vine to which we are tied through Judah. He is the beautiful and glorious fruit-bearing branch **(Isaiah 4:2)**.

Nothing could be more stealthy or cunning than the act played out on the altar of Calvary. Here is the ultimate in traumatic occasions. The Master is gone. The One so many had followed is dead. There He hangs for all people of all time to see. Who cannot ponder on this act without envisioning the terrible sign of Jesus crucified?

Hell was going wild. Demons were ecstatically dancing in the streets of hell. The world was elated. The carnal traditional religionists had won the battle. Jesus Christ, that upstart who claimed to be the Messiah, that revolutionist of Israel who even claimed to be God, was dead!

And then, all of a sudden, He was back and He was alive! He had the keys to death, hell and the grave. He had possibly lost a battle, but now all the world is learning that Jesus Christ, truly a man, truly God, and truly the Redeemer of mankind, Who has risen back to life, has won the war. Nothing is more stealthy or cunning. Jesus Christ is truly the Lion of Judah. He is God's bow. Zechariah says God will bend it and fill with Ephraim.

EPHRAIM, STRENGTH OF ISRAEL, POINTS TO THE GENTILES

Now Ephraim was not a son of Jacob, he was the younger son of Joseph. Manassah was the firstborn. As Joseph set his sons at the knees of his father, his father reached forward to them. Joseph tried to correct him. Joseph had strategically placed them in such away that his father's right hand would rest upon the head of Manassah, his firstborn. But Jacob crossed his hands and refused to be corrected by Joseph. Ephraim thereby received the blessing Joseph desired for Manassah.

Ephraim is a wild bull ox. He multiplies at a phenomenal rate. He violently brings truth to the lost. The wildness of Ephraim is like the wildness of the olive branch Romans 2 speaks of as Paul refers first to the remnant—the loyal few of Israel who refuse to bow to Baal, and then to the Gentile, whom he compares to a wild shoot grafted into the good olive tree. This shoot then shares in the nourishing sap coming from the root or the source of nourishment —the truth of God's Holy Word.

The Gentile replaces those branches which were lopped off because of unbelief. Ephraim represents this replacement. His attribute of violently bringing truth to the lost can be associated with the statement of Jesus when he said the violent take the kingdom by force **(Matthew 11:12)**. If you are prepared to fight in the spirit to take back the property stolen by Satan, then you can find a rightful place in the Body of Christ, through the attributes of Ephraim.

Phenomenal growth can most readily be associated with the fullness of God's Holy Spirit freely manifested in the world. When the Holy Spirit came down on the day of Pentecost, the Body that had shrunk to 120 was immediately increased to 3000 as the convicting power was manifested **(Acts 2:41)**.

GROWTH IN THE SPIRIT

Tremendous growth occurred for about 25 years as the church gave the Holy Spirit full freedom. But then, as the record of history shows, the organized church exchanged the spontaneity of the Spirit's guidance for the guidance of men, governing and conducting itself like any other power-hungry worldly organization. The sins that accompanied desire for power and control over others opened the door wide for Satan to enter the church. The Reformation and the rise of Protestantism changed little. The controlling spirit was still in the church, holding the door open for all of his friends from hell. Real change only came with the approach of the twentieth century, when men in numbers again began receiving the power of God through the baptism in the Holy Spirit.

At no time in the history of the church has there been growth like the present. It has recently been estimated that one out of four of those who call themselves Christians are moving into the fullness of the first fruits of God's glory **(Romans 8:23)**.

MAN IN GOD'S BOW

Zechariah says that God will fill the bow of Judah with the arrow of Ephraim. So, if Judah is Jesus, the bow, and Ephraim is the spirit-filled Christian, the arrow, then the uniting of man into God—in God's quest to free man from Satan and to establish His kingdom by forcefully removing the believer and the earth from the ensnaring grasp of Satan—is now in place.

THE SPIRIT WILL STEER YOU

The bow is bent, aimed and loaded with the arrow by the Holy Spirit. God has prepared man for battle. Now lastly He arms him with the sword of the mighty warrior **(Zechariah 9:13)**.

Because of God's everlasting blood covenant of commitment to regenerated reconciliation, man is restored to his rightful authority, power and domain in Christ Jesus. He is freed from the waterless pit by being filled with the inundating power of the Holy Spirit to witness boldly to the world as he grasps the Sword of the Spirit—the Word of God **(Ephesians 6:17)**.

He is now raised up from on high as a son of Zion to come against the sons of Greece **(Zechariah 9:13)**. The Church is overthrowing Satan by the blood of the Lamb and by it's testimony **(Revelation 12:11)**. It is loaded as an arrow into the bow of Judah, stretched and aimed as a joint heir in Christ Jesus and launched forth as the Body of Christ into the fullness of Him which fills all things or, as the New International version says, fills the universe **(Ephesians 1:23, 4:10)**.

YOUR COOPERATION HELPS IN YOUR DELIVERANCE

Eve once had a woman bring her sister and her mother for prayer. I was nearby attending a meeting. The sister seemed quite introverted, perhaps mildly retarded, and could not talk well. She said that she wanted to talk that "funny talk" she heard others speaking in church, and so Eve prayed with her. She gave her life to Christ and received the baptism in the Holy Ghost. She got her wish—she spoke in tongues. She also had her tongue released for natural speech and later became far more free and was comfortably active in church and social affairs.

The mother was presented as very mean. She used foul language and did not believe in heaven or hell. Eve prayed for her, holding her hands and speaking love to her. Although the old lady spoke hardly any English at all she looked back at Eve and said "I love you."

When Eve began to pray for the woman who had brought her sister and mother to be counseled (who, herself, in reality had been sent by her husband), Eve discerned powerful spirits, so she asked me to assist her. Let's call this woman Anabelle.

The trauma from her mother's hatred and abuse brought forth the spirits of rejection and jealousy, as well as spirits of murder, hatred and suicide. Several times the strongman spirit in her had spoken to her inner being, telling her to kill her husband. It also punished her by slapping her face, choking her and pulling her hair. Even more astoundingly, it burned and bit her skin. She actually had highly visible marks on her body that would remain for days from the attacks by the demon upon her body.

Anabelle attacked her husband with a knife. She hit him in the head with a large coffee mug, and on one occasion she woke up in bed to find him covered in blood from her attack.

Three times the suicide spirit had attempted to get her to kill herself. She tried to resist these orders to kill but she could not. She took an entire bottle of sleeping pills on three different occasions. The reason she did not die is because she cried out to God each time to save her and He did!

Before taking authority over those vicious spirits, we led Anabelle in prayer. We had her repent of her sins and recommit her life to Christ. We had her rebuke the devil in Jesus' name and then we gave her instructions. We told her to keep her eyes open at all times while we prayed. We encouraged her to believe that she would be set free, and we told her to trust Jesus and nothing else.

As we began praying her cooperation helped greatly. The spirit kept trying to get her to close her eyes and go to sleep.

They hide in this way. Sometimes when people are slain in the spirit, demons use the occasion to hide and remain. This is why the spiritual gift of discerning of spirits is so important. This in no manner or form is intended to question or challenge the validity of being slain in the spirit. It simply approaches the isolated incidents when Satan gets involved as a counterfeiter.

The spirits left as we commanded them to in Jesus' name. Anabelle is a totally different person today. She is no longer introverted or nonsocial. She smiles often (which she seldom did prior to that prayer session). She is active in church affairs. She is no longer fearful, and her husband says that their relationship and her spiritual relationship with God are greatly improved.

LONG DISTANCE DELIVERANCE

A woman we had been ministering to called one Wednesday afternoon for prayer. Although it was right at supper time, the weather was bad, and we had responded to her calls numerous times in just the last few days, I discerned the need for more deliverance. I started to pray for her, but she stopped me. She insisted that I come back to her home right then but I refused.

I told her the demon could be cast out over the phone. She disputed my statement. She insisted that I would have to lay hands on her for the demon to go. I told her the demon was gone, regardless of what she may have thought or believed. She made a few disgruntled statements and hung up the phone.

That night she accompanied her family to a church they had never attended before. The pastor interrupted the service to call her out of the congregation. He said, "Sister, I have a word for you. The Lord would have me tell you that you are clean."

One evening a very young child called on the phone. Eve could not understand what he was saying and she did not recognize the voice. She assumed the child had dialed a wrong number but yet she still told him to call back later.

The child had been calling for his mother who could not hear well. She then went to a neighbor and had the neighbor call for her. She told Eve she was hearing voices and that she had discolored bruises on her body from demonic attacks. Eve made an appointment for her to come for counseling and then prayed for her over the phone. I was on the extension supporting her with prayer in the spirit.

After Eve prayed I asked her how she felt. She said there was something in her throat and something was moving around in her body. Eve prayed again.

Then I asked her to put her neighbor back on the line. The neighbor said she choked violently and spit up something, and was calm after that. Distance is not a problem with the power of prayer. Jesus marveled at the faith of the Centurion who told him he need not make the journey to his servant. "Just speak the word and he will be healed."

CHAPTER 11

TRAUMA CAN OPEN THE WAY FOR GOD

Elijah is another who suffered great trauma. His trauma came as Jezebel the ungodly queen of King Ahab threatened him with death. His trauma came following a great spiritual victory which he won before Jezebel's priests of Baal, the king and the people of Israel **(1 Kings 18:20-39)**.

JEZEBEL: A THREATENING MURDEROUS SPIRIT

Ahab the king who did more evil in the eyes of the Lord than any king before him **(1 Kings 16:30)** married Jezebel. She was a Sidonian Princess who killed the Lord's prophets **(1 Kings 18:4)**. She was so evil that Jesus, in addressing his charges against the church of Thyatira through John on Patmos, uses her name in identifying the spirit which is responsible for leading the church into fornication, idolatry and false teaching **(Revelation 2:20)**.

Elijah prophesied a drought on Israel to Ahab. Elijah was fed by ravens alongside the Kerith Ravine, from which he drank until the brook dried up. He then moved to the home of a widow and her sons. She was down to their last meal, until he spoke a miracle over her empty pantry, which then fed them for the duration of the famine. He even prayed one of her dead sons back to life. All of this is told in 1 Kings 17.

THE MANIFEST PRESENCE EXPOSES
SATAN'S USE OF TRAUMA

Then Elijah confronted Ahab and the priests of Baal on Mount Carmel. He challenged the people to stop wavering between two opinions. He charged them to follow one and drop the other, but the people could not answer him. They had no response. They said nothing **(1 Kings 18:20-21)**. They were as Elijah charged, without an opinion. This made them pliable. Drop your manmade opinions and give God freedom in your life. Give Him freedom to work in your heart and you will see Him perform signs and wonders on your life.

He gave the priests of Baal several hours to call their gods down to consume their sacrifice. Then he stepped forward. He called out to God and fire came down from heaven. The people could then speak. They were freed from their bondage. They fell prostrate and cried aloud "the Lord—he is the God. The Lord—he is the God." **(I Kings 18:22-39)** They had seen the wonders of God. They knew now what to say.

Then Elijah killed all of the pagan priests. Israel had received deliverance from the trauma of trying to serve two gods. Elijah spoke the end to the famine and rain returned to the land. As Ahab returned to Jezebel Elijah ran on foot faster than the horses could draw the chariot of Ahab **(1 Kings 18:40-46)**.

Ahab went home and told his wife Jezebel of all that Elijah had done. Instead of being humbled and enthusiastic over this wonderful transformation of their nation she vowed to kill Elijah within twenty-four hours (1 Kings 19:1-2). This threat brought trauma to the mind of Elijah.

TRAUMA CHANGES ONE'S WAY OF THINKING

In a relatively brief period of time, Elijah had done a heroic number of prodigious feats, all by the Spirit of God. He stopped the rain from falling, was fed by birds, filled the widow's barrow and resurrected her son from death, faced down a death threat from the king, destroyed an entire national satanic religion, called fire down from heaven, converted an entire nation and outran a horsedrawn chariot. Elijah had no logical reason to fear anything!

But trauma is a dynamic force. It is an experience extremely hard to reckon with. It is an encounter which calls for God's help.

GO TO THE SOURCE

He is your most certain source. He will bring you through. You need not succumb to the attacks of Satan's demons. They are just sitting, watching and waiting for an opportunity to move in. But you can resist them with a Power far greater than theirs!

DEMONS—DISEMBODIED SPIRITS

Demons are evil spirits without bodies who spend their every moment looking for a body to make into a valley of dry bones. This is their obsession, which they pursue with an expertise very close to perfection. It is a work performed by personalities in the spirit realm, far superior to the carnal-based abilities of the human who naturally resists the desire of Christ Jesus to move him into the realm of the spirit and to fill him with the power to put these demons under his feet **(Ephesians 1:22)**.

THE FLESH WEAKENS THE SPIRIT

As trauma struck Elijah, he caved in and opened up to spiritual attack. The spirit of fear set in **(1 Kings 19:3)**. God had gifted Elijah with all sorts of victories. He was absolutely invincible to any force which could come at him from any source. But he was still encased in what Paul calls a tent, a house or a tabernacle **(2 Corinthians 5:1-2)**. He says we groan, earnestly desiring to be clothed upon with our house which is in heaven. Our mortal body is weak and susceptible to the inroads of demonic activity.

Elijah's flesh was weak. His spirit overcame great enemies, but when the flesh overruled he ran in utter panic. He went off into the desert and sat down under a broom tree, utterly depressed. Fear gripped him so strongly he was ready to give up and die **(1 Kings 19:3-5)**.

GOD STRENGTHENS BY HIS SPIRIT

God strengthened him by having the Angel of the Lord feed him. He rested and then the Lord served him another meal. Elijah then traveled forty days and forty nights through the wilderness on the Lord's meals **(1 Kings 19:6-8)**. This is reminiscent of Israel traveling forty years in the Lord's care before entering the Promised Land.

It is also indicative of *our* walk through life. Jesus says it is not by bread alone but by the Word of God **(Luke 4:4)**. Zechariah says it is not by might or by power but by the spirit says the Lord **(Zechariah 4:6)**. You need to be spiritually strong at all times. You need to be strengthened by the bread of the Word **(Luke 4:4)**. You need to grow in the spirit **(2 Peter 3:18 KJV)**. You need to pray in the spirit **(Jude 20)**. Satan will attack when you least expect, however, you can be certain that his attack will come through trauma or temptation. You can also be assured that God will be prepared to help you. He will bring you through if you are in His will.

GO BACK THE WAY YOU CAME

When Elijah reached the end of his journey God spoke to him in a still, small, gentle, whispering voice. God told him to go back the way he came **(1 Kings 19:12-15)**.

CORRECT YOUR ERRORS

Oftentimes this is the answer. Face up to what you are running from. Face up to what has got hold of you. Stop and go to the master's table. Refresh yourself with the children's Bread. Reach up to the table or scrounge beneath it, but get it. It's yours to have. Whatever your need, God's Word can meet it.

FACE YOUR FEARS AND TRAUMAS, HEAD ON

Elijah went back the way he came. He anointed two kings and a successor for himself. He crossed the Jordan with dry feet and entered heaven without tasting death **(1 Kings 19:15, 2 Kings 2:11)**. The threats he fearfully ran from never manifested. God did not allow the words of Jezebel to be fulfilled.

Go back the way you came. Go back to that trauma. Go back and close the door. Go back and break the curse. Go back and sever the bindings. Go back and face that devil in Jesus' name, and drive him out forever. Give him back double everything he's done to you **(Revelation 18:8)**. Take back everything he's stolen from you. Take it back double **(Job 42:10)**. And you can count on the Lord to make the way for your returning steps of reconciliation and restitution.

When the Lord provided for us to settle in Mississippi, we built a home on some former farm land Eve's parents gave us out of the goodness of their hearts. After moving in I ordered a portable utility shed. I had it placed adjacent to a stack of concrete blocks left over from the construction work. I used a weed eater to clear the area for the delivery of the shed. As I was cutting the grass that had grown up around the blocks I experienced trauma. I felt the unmistakable pain of a striking snake hit the ankle of my left leg. I had read an article years earlier about a woman being bitten by a snake in her garden. It felt just like she described it.

I immediately turned and looked for the snake. As I did I spoke Mark 16:17-18 out loud. However, I found nothing. The shed was delivered the next morning. As the workman was setting it up he called me over. He showed me two copperhead snakes, male and female, coiled up inside one of the concrete blocks. He had a gun and shot them both.

YOU CAN CLOSE THE DOOR

Except for a sore ankle, there were no aftereffects at all from the bite. Although trauma is a doorway for Satan's entry, he does not need to be allowed in. The Word will stop him. The anointing breaks the yoke. The blood seals off his entry.

The night before the exodus, the death angel passed over Egypt. It was a night of great trauma. Following the dictates of God, Moses had all of Israel apply blood to their door posts and lintels. Not one Hebrew child died that night. Satan cannot cross the blood line.

HE WILL DO WHAT YOU ASK OF HIM

When Jesus cast the Legion of spirits from the Gadarene they went into the pigs. The townspeople then came out to the scene. They saw the man who had spent many nights screaming naked in their cemetery. He had broken the links when they tried to chain him. They now saw the man calm, dressed and delivered.

What should have been joy for them turned into trauma. They could not handle this wondrous sign from God in their community. They ordered Jesus to leave. He did. He got back in the boat with his disciples and left.

When Jesus approached his disciples walking on the surface of the water in the midst of a terrible storm, they experienced trauma. The storm did not bother them. They were accustomed to storms on the lake. They could not, however, handle what they presumed to be a ghost as they observed Jesus walking past them atop the water.

Peter stepped out of the boat and followed him until he became fearful of the wind. Peter called for Jesus to save him, and He did.

Then the rest of the disciples, who had remained in their trauma in the boat, called out to Jesus. They asked Him to get in the boat with them. He did. As he stepped into the boat the storm stopped and they and the boat were instantaneously translated three miles to the shore.

In each instance Jesus did what was asked of Him. He left when He was asked to do so. He allowed Peter to follow Him when Peter asked Him, and He got in the boat with the disciples when they invited Him.

He will do the same for you. In your time of trauma you can tell Jesus to leave and demons will pounce on you. You can ask Him to allow you to follow Him and he will receive you. You can invite Him to come and join you in your storm of life and he will do just that.

HE WILL TRANSLATE YOU
OUT OF THE STORM

He will change your life. He will transform your trauma to expectant joy. He will fill you with his Holy Spirit and translate you into the ecstasy of His truth, power, faith, hope, and love.

TRAUMA ITSELF WILL NOT DESTROY

Mary His mother undoubtedly experienced all of this. She seems to have lived a life of trauma. From the time the angel first appeared to her to announce the overwhelming news that she had been selected to mother God's own son, trauma clearly overshadowed her life.

The problem of having no proper or decent place to give birth had to have been traumatic. Leaving home in the night amidst the screams and cries of mothers losing their infant children as Herod's soldiers searched to slay her Son was enough to shake the sanity of anyone. She had to search three days for Him in Jerusalem. He was constantly rejected by His own family, neighbors, and even the religious leaders. She had to see Him arrested, falsely tried, beaten, dragged naked through town, hung on that terrible cross and, finally, she had to watch Him die. The trauma was unquestionably more than most would ever have to face.

But Mary had so much to lean on. The visit from Gabriel in itself was enough to give her the strength to sustain the traumas which followed. She saw Him sit and astound the elders at age twelve with His spiritual wisdom. She saw them astounded by His wisdom and power as He went forth in His anointed, Spirit-filled ministry. She quite confidently told the servants to do what He would tell them to do prior to His first miracle. She saw Him risen from the grave and she was present to receive the Holy Spirit on Pentecost.

THE INFILLING CAN SHATTER
TRAUMA AND ITS EFFECTS

This event alone was enough to shatter all the trauma of her past life. It was enough to drive every demon on earth from her door. It was enough to fill her with peace and unspeakable joy. As those tongues of fire settled on the heads of each of them in that upper room, as they all began speaking in tongues and reeling under the power of the Holy Spirit, she had the absolute assurance that what He had promised to do was done.

Jesus told them He was going to heaven. He said that when He got there He would send the Holy Spirit back. The presence of the INFILLING and the signs and wonders it produces is confirmation that Jesus Christ is on the throne.

GOD HONORS LAW

Mary Magdalene, Mary the mother of James, and Salome approached the tomb of Jesus, according to the account of the resurrection as told by Mark **(Mark 16:1-3)**. They faced considerable trauma. They had seen the Master slain. They had gone through the customary wailing, and now they were approaching the tomb with spices to anoint the body of Christ—however, they had a considerable problem.

As they went, they wondered how the stone would be rolled away for them to enter. Some translations say they wondered who would roll the stone away. The Living Bible says they wondered how they would be able to roll the stone away. Consummately, this is trauma in itself.

These women went out to perform a task they could not perform. They went to anoint the entombed dead body of Jesus Christ with absolutely no way of reaching that dead body. No one could remove that stone and, even if they could, it would have been against the law to do so. Not only was the stone impossible for the women themselves to move, every law there is prohibited it's being moved.

The laws of nature would not allow the stone to move itself. The law of the land prohibited moving the stone. The order, the seal and the guard held that stone in place. Divine law also was in effect because God honors the laws of nature and man. He commands that law be obeyed.

PRECEDENT SUPERCEDES LAW

Unless a precedent or a superseding law can be found, a law remains binding. This is a principal of law. So not even God would move the stone. It appeared that Satan would finally win. Jesus, however, had prophesied that He would return after three days. Other scriptures predicted his resurrection.

The superseding law of God's Word prevails over all other law. This fact enabled the stone to move. Although no man could move the stone, the Holy Spirit had authority in line with the Word, and He brought Jesus back to life **(Romans 8:11)**.

That stone stood in the way of your resurrection as well as that of Jesus's. It prohibited your salvation. It enabled Satan to prevail. Jesus says that if you will stand on the rock, Satan cannot prevail. The stone was an obstacle, but the Rock is its master! You tell that stone, that mountain, that trauma, that demon in your life to get lost. Tell it to go, in the Name of Jesus, the Rock on which you stand. It must and it will go! Call upon the Lord and he will answer you. Isaiah 65:24 says He will answer even before you call.

Once, while watching the Trinity Broadcasting Network on television, I saw a remarkable thing. A Catholic Priest was preaching when a high powered light bulb exploded right in his face. Particles of glass immediately penetrated his eye. Instantly the priest grabbed his eye in obvious pain.

THE APPLE OF HIS EYE

The eye is one of the most sensitive parts of the body. The lens of the eye is known as the "apple" of the eye. God says you are the apple of *His* eye **(Zechariah 2:8)**. This means you are the most sensitive part of Him. He will protect you first.

REACT INSTANTLY TO TRAUMA

As the priest grabbed his injured eye he simultaneously called out "Jesus! Jesus!" The scene was shown and reshown several times across the network for millions to see. The reason this was so remarkable to me was that he was able to instantly cry out. He faced trauma with an instant cry to Jesus for help. He was heard, and he was healed. I pray that I would be able to respond as quickly, the next time I face trauma.

The challenge comes because trauma is seldom antici-pated. It almost always arrives unexpected. Satan always has a demon waiting to come in when trauma comes. He wants to unleash as much upheaval in your life as he can get away with. However, you can slam the door in his face before he makes his entry, and even if he does get in you can cast him back out, in the Name of Jesus!

The third chapter of the Book of Revelation tells you that Jesus is standing at the door knocking. He is more faithful to you than the demon is to Satan. Just open the door to Jesus and He will come in and sup with you. He will strengthen you. He will prepare you to react adequately to your next trauma.

OTHER BOOKS FROM THESE AUTHORS

MINISTERING DELIVERANCE

Simple explanations of the Scriptural basis for demonic activity in addition to means for avoiding such activity and effectively negating it as provided by God.

Available at local Christian Bookstores
or
you may order from
Impact Christian Books,
1-800-451-2708
or call **Flaming Sword Ministries'** prayer line
1-601-365-7731

GROWTH GUIDE FOR FAITH WARRIORS

Two part seven volume Spiritual Warfare Manual for those who want a deeper understanding and walk in the Spirit. (Includes follow up guidance by correspondence.)

Order this directly from:

Flaming Sword Ministries
P.O. Box 159,
Baldwyn, MS 38824
1-601-365-7731

FOR ADDITIONAL COPIES WRITE:

Impac
Chris **ian**
Books

332 Leffingwell Ave., Suite 101
Kirkwood, MO 63122

AVAILABLE AT YOUR LOCAL BOOKSTORE, OR YOU MAY
ORDER DIRECTLY. Toll-Free, order-line only M/C, DISC,
or VISA 1-800-451-2708.